Deviant Fertility in China

Deviant Fertility in China

Li Li

NOVA SCIENCE PUBLISHERS, INC.
Commack, NY

Creative Design: Gavin Aghamore

Editorial Production: Susan Boriotti

Assistant Vice President/Art Director: Maria Ester Hawrys

Office Manager: Annette Hellinger

Graphics: Frank Grucci

Manuscript Coordinator: Phyllis Gaynor

Book Production: Joanne Bennette, Michelle Keller, Ludmila Kwartiroff, Christine Mathosian, Joanne Metal, Tammy Sauter and Tatiana Shohov

Circulation: Iyatunde Abdullah, Sharon Britton, and Cathy DeGregory

Library of Congress Cataloging-in-Publication Data
available upon request

ISBN 1-56072-445-5

Copyright © 1997 by   Nova Science Publishers, Inc.
6080 Jericho Turnpike, Suite 207
Commack, New York 11725
Tele. 516-499-3103   Fax 516-499-3146
E-Mail: Novascience@earthlink.net

Printed in the United States of America

To Xiang Chen,

my "ultimate classmate",

to learn and grow together.

CONTENTS

ACKNOWLEDGMENTS

This manuscript is a revised vision of my Ph.D. dissertation written in 1992. I would like to express my appreciation to many individuals with whom I have shared my experience as a graduate student at Virginia Tech. Foremost, I wish to sincerely thank my advisor, Dr. John Ballweg. His constant encouragement, inspiration, and invaluable aids make my graduate training a significant learning process. I will be always grateful for his energetic directions and help during my M.S. and Ph.D. programs. I also want to thank Dr. Clifton D. Bryant, Dr. Cornelia B. Flora, Dr. Theodore D. Fuller, and Dr. Paul D. Metz, for their continuing assistance and constructive criticisms. Their contributions for this study are truly recognized and appreciated.

I am indebted to many friends who form a warm and understanding support group for me. I want to thank JiangTao Li for assisting me in data collection in China. Special thanks go to my friends, Shu and Q. J., who let me shelter in their apartment to finish my study.

I want to thank my parents, for providing me with much encouragement in my education and confidence in my success. Finally, this manuscript is dedicated to my husband, Xiang Chen. Without his support and understanding, the completion of this manuscript would have been impossible.

LIST OF ILLUSTRATIONS

CHAPTER I

INTRODUCTION

The People's Republic of China, the most populous nation in the world, has witnessed an extraordinary fertility decline during the last two decades, with its total fertility rate (TFR) falling from 5.81 in 1970 to 2.25 in 1989 (Greenhalgh, 1989; People's Daily, 1991). This fertility decline is unprecedented not only in the history of China, but also among all large-size populations ever in human history (Wang, 1987; Lavely, 1986). The Chinese government estimates that approximately 200 million births have been avoided since 1971 (People's Daily, 1990).

This remarkable achievement has stimulated a heated debate on factors contributing to such a rapid fertility decline. Given that China is a predominantly agricultural developing country, the role of socioeconomic development in China's fertility transition remains controversial (Kaufman, 1983; Tien, 1984; Poston and Gu, 1987; Wang, 1988). There is little doubt among scholars, however, that the family planning programs initiated and organized by the Chinese government are the major factors responsible for the fertility transition in China (Mauldin, 1982; Qian, 1983).

While many Western and Chinese scholars highly regard the success of the Chinese family planning programs, some recently released data are revealing. According to the 1990 Population Census of China, the overall proportion of first-child births in 1989 were slightly less than one-half (49.51%) of all births of that year. About 31.7% of the total births in 1989 were second-child births, and some 19.32% of children born in 1989 were third or even higher order births in their families (People's Daily, 1991; Population Census Office, 1991). Several other studies also uncovered similar results. For example, it was found that high parity births, including second and higher parities, accounted for 34.19% of the total births in 1986. In 1988 only about 10% of women in the childbearing age received one child certificates[1] (Ye, 1991). Peng Peiyun, Minister-in-Charge of the State Family Planning Commission, admitted that the national population growth would surpass the target of the family planning program, as the "out-of-plan"[2] births in the next five years would reach approximately 14 million (People's Daily, 1989). In fact, many Chinese couples have more children than the number the government "plans" for them, despite that they are facing various normative pressures and punishments.

Sociologically speaking, those couples who have more children than "planned" deviate from current reproductive norms, which have been enforced through the family planning campaigns and conformed to by many Chinese couples. This deviation, or "deviant fertility," is a unique social phenomenon existing in contemporary China and is a significant topic of sociological inquiries, not only for the future implementation of population policy, but also for understanding of Chinese reproductive behavior in general. Yet few studies, if any, have been done in this regard.

This manuscript contributes to a better understanding of "deviant fertility" in China. To do so, this study attempts to pursue the following objectives:

---

[1] One child certificates are issued by the Chinese government to those couples who have only one child and promise not to have any more in the future.

[2] "Out-of-plan birth" or "out-of-plan fertility" is the term used by the Chinese government and the public to refer to the births that exceed the number being authorized by the government, although these births may be planned by the parents.

1) conceptualize the "out-of-plan" fertility in China in a theoretical framework that incorporates sociology of fertility with deviant behavior perspectives.

2) establish research models, based upon the conceptual framework developed, to identify relevant variables and to illustrate behavior patterns in their social contexts.

3) understand the "out-of-plan" fertility by examining its determinants with comparison to its "planned" counterpart.

CHAPTER II

LITERATURE REVIEW

"Deviant fertility" is surely a new issue in population studies. Yet inquiries into this topic cannot be accomplished by totally deviating from previous studies in the area of fertility, especially previous studies of demands for children. In fact, it seems logical to assume that those couples in China who want to have their "out-of-plan" children essentially have very strong demands for children, which constitute a precondition of deviant fertility. In this regard, previous studies of demands for children will be the central focus in this literature review.

In the past few decades, the topic of demands for children has attracted hundreds, if not thousands, of scientific studies. This academic interest is primarily stimulated by the threats of population growth to mankind's welfare, in developed and developing countries. The abundant theories and schools of thought in this field are classified into three basic categories: economic, psychological, and sociological theories, though overlaps among them may exist. The main purpose of this section is to review writings that fall into these three traditions.

ECONOMIC PERSPECTIVES

Generally speaking, an economic theory starts with the postulate that rational self-interested people choose to consume the goods that give them the greatest satisfaction. Individual fertility behavior, therefore, has its rationale that tends to maximize the utility function through fertility decision-making as responses to economic resource constraints. Based on this assumption, a number of economists examined demands for children in terms of family production and consumption, the cost and quality of children, the allocation of human time and capital, and household utility functions (Becker, 1960, 1965, 1988; Turchi, 1975; Easterlin, 1975, 1978; Jones, 1982; Leibenstein, 1957, 1975, 1980; Schultz, 1974; Willis, 1973).

In 1957, Harvey Leibenstein, in his book *Economic Backwardness and Economic Growth*, made an initial attempt to examine how couples want to have children from a micro-economic perspective (Leibenstein, 1957). Three years later, Gary Becker applied a traditional consumer-decision theory to analyze demands for children (Becker, 1960). Since these two pioneering studies, economic research on the topic of fertility has mushroomed. Basically, these economic studies fall into two major schools of thoughts: the Chicago School (the new household economics or demand theory) approach and the socioeconomic approach (Jones, 1982; Sanderson, 1976). The former is largely identified with Becker and his colleagues at the University of Chicago and Columbia (Becker, 1965, 1988; Schultz, 1974), while the latter is primarily represented by the studies of Leibenstein (1957, 1975, 1980) and Easterlin (1975, 1978).

The Chicago school rests on its micro-economic premise that, for a married couple, children are durable goods as any other commodities, yielding utility to the parents and requiring inputs to produce. Thus, fertility behavior is regarded as both a consuming and producing behavior. A family is a decision-making unit that, according to the Chicago school, maximizes its utility in consumption as well as in allocating time and goods in production activities. Since childbearing and childrearing are very time-consuming, if a couple chooses to have children, they must weigh the rewards from bearing and rearing children against rewards from other activities. Accordingly, an increase in the cost for raising children or an increase in the opportunity cost, such as employment opportunities for women, will reduce the number of children desired by parents. Furthermore, demands for children concern not only the quantity of children but the "quality" of children as well. In this regard, couples with higher income might not desire larger family sizes but better quality of children instead (Becker, 1960, 1965, 1988; Jones, 1982; Schultz, 1974; Willis, 1974).

The socioeconomic approach attempts to build an economic theory of fertility by taking social status, tastes, supplies, and demographic transitions into account. The socioeconomic explanation focuses on the relationship between social status and tastes, and its impact on demands for children. According to Leibenstein, the tastes of an individual are directly determined by his or her socioeconomic status, including education, occupation, and other characteristics. As a consequence of economic changes, the tastes for children also change. Because economic changes bring about a great increase in the expenditure on status identification and a rise in the cost of children, the demand for children will decline (Leibenstein, 1957, 1975). Easterlin (1975, 1978) further argued that not only tastes but also "supply" factors should be emphasized. In societies where most of the population is subject to natural fertility, differences in achieved fertility may just reflect natural fecundity rather than desired family sizes. This mechanism, however, may not be applicable to groups who deliberately regulate their fertility (Easterlin, 1975, 1978). From this starting point, the supply-demand framework integrates three components, the demand for children, the supply of children, and fertility regulation cost, into a single analysis (Bulatao and Lee, 1983; Easterlin, 1985).

Both the Chicago school and the socioeconomic approach place their main emphases on the economic considerations of costs and benefits of fertility. Their similarities as well as differences are summarized by Jones (1982) as follows:

The two main schools in the economics of fertility differ mainly with regard to how narrowly economic is the focus of their model. The Chicago School hews to a rigorously economic, income-and-prices framework with the couple as the unit of analysis, and it stands or falls on the "quality of children" argument in explaining the declining demand for children as income rise. By allowing an explanatory role for shift in tastes, the socioeconomic school is more open to the insights of sociology and psychology and has greater potential for explaining the forces making for high fertility in many developing countries and the timing of the onset of fertility decline. Its model, however, becomes more complex and less readily testable (Jones, 1982: 285).

SOCIO-PSYCHOLOGICAL PERSPECTIVES

Similar to the economic perspective, the psychological approach also assumes behavioral rationality and utility maximation. However, while micro-economists simply assume a process of rational maximation of utility, psychological theorists go further to describe the process in detail and to capture more complexity in reproductive behavior. Although several variants of the theory can be discerned in the literature, they share some basic assumptions. They assume that reproductive behavior of individual couples largely depend on their individual behavioral tendencies. Accordingly, psychological studies focus on individual motivations, attitudes, perceptions, personalities, and decisions, which are critical to understanding human fertility (Fawcett, 1970; Rosenstiel, et al., 1980).

An important contribution of the psychological perspective to the knowledge of demands for children is its systematic examination of individual motives for and against childbearing with respect to the value of children. According to Hoffman and Hoffman (1973), the value of children refers to the functions they serve or the needs they fulfill for parents. They assert that the motivation to have a child depends on the value of the child to the individual. The value of children is further conceptualized in the following categories (Hoffman and Hoffman, 1973: 46-47):

1. Adult status and social identity;
2. Expansion of the self-tie to a larger entity, "immortality";

3. Morality: religion; altruism; good of the group; norms regarding sexuality, impulsivity, virtue;
4. Primary group ties, affiliation;
5. Stimulation, novelty, fun;
6. Creativity, accomplishment, competence;
7. Power, influence, effectance;
8. Social comparison, competition;
9. Economic utility.

In this way, Hoffman's model illustrates various ways in which children may be valued by their parents. Differentiated from economic models with quantified costs and benefits of children from economic data, psychologists deal with the value of children with respect to the ways parents perceive children. Following this tradition, many researches on the value of children have been conducted in different countries and cultures (Bulatao, 1982; Bulatao and Arnold, 1977; Buripakdi, 1977; Hoffman and Manis, 1979; Iritani, 1979; Lee and Kim, 1977; Wu, 1977).

Another contribution from the psychological perspective consists in theories of attitudes, proposed by Fishbein and his colleagues (Fishbein 1967, 1972; Fishbein and Jaccard, 1973). According to Fishbein's model, fertility, like other human behaviors, is determined by the intention of an individual to perform that behavior. The individual's intention to perform fertility behavior can be predicted by (1) one's attitude toward the fertility behavior and (2) one's normative beliefs obtained from others regarding the behavior. An individual's attitude toward performing fertility behavior is a function of his or her beliefs in the consequences of the behavior and the evaluation of those consequences (Fishbein and Jaccard, 1973; Pagel and Davidson, 1984). In this model an individual's personal attitudes and societal normative constraints are the joint factors of fertility behavior. Yet norms may or may not be important depending upon personal attitudes and intentions (Fishbein, 1972). For many years the Fishbein model has been widely used in fertility studies and has received a great deal of empirical support (Jaccard and Davidson, 1972; Pagel and Davidson, 1984; Vinokur-Kaplan, 1978; Werner, et al., 1975).

Theories of decision making also make contributions for studying human fertility. Various models in this area share a general assumption that individuals' choices are determined by their estimation of the consequences that could result from their decision making. In theory, individuals should take the act if the expected value of engaging in the act exceeds the expected value of not doing so. In this regard the probability of having children is seen as a function of the ratio of perceived advantages and disadvantages of the behavior (Adler, 1979; Pagel and Davidson, 1984). The subjective expected utility is one of the models that is used frequently in fertility studies. This model explicitly views fertility choices as decisions between having and not having a child. The choice involves an overall evaluation of the many consequences (positive/negative; pleasant/unpleasant; good/bad) of each option (Burch, 1980). As Adler writes,

Decision makers behave as though they compared the outcomes of various alternatives, choosing the one with the highest subjective expected utility (Adler, 1979: 188).

Some direct applications of the model are provided by the studies of Beach and colleagues (1976), Townes and associates (1977, 1980), and Thomson (1984).

SOCIOLOGICAL PERSPECTIVES

In broad terms, sociological perspectives of fertility attempt to identify the social determinants of demands for children. Differentiated from the economic and the psychological perspectives that use individuals as the unit of analysis, sociologists focus on the whole society or groups within the society. In Freedman's words:

The problem is not why one couple rather than another is at a particular place in the frequency distribution of births in a society, but why the society as a whole has the particular frequency distribution that distinguishes it from another (Freedman, 1975: 10).

Another key feature of the sociological perspective lies in its stress on social institutions, social norms, or cultures, which are believed to govern individual fertility expectations and behavior (Davis, 1959; Freedman, 1975; Hawthorn, 1970). In addition, fertility trends in a society are not divorced from the level of socioeconomic development or modernization in that society. In other words, changes in demands for children are associated with the process of modernization. Sociological theories concerning demands for children can be further grouped into three categories: the demographic transition theory, the social institution theory, and the normative theory.

The Demographic Transition Theory

The demographic transition theory was first proposed by Warren Thompson in 1929, and a full formulation of the theory was put forward by Frank Notestein in 1945 (Thompson, 1929; Notestein, 1945). In its "classic" form the theory is a descriptive interpretation of demographic changes that took place in 19th-century Europe. Specifically, it describes the transition from high birth rates and death rates to low birth rates and death rates, and views the transformation as a result of a decline in mortality, particularly infant mortality, and an improvement in social and economic conditions (Notestein, 1945; van de Walle and Knodel, 1980). For many years the demographic transition theory has been considered as an ideal pattern that might be applied to other places including developing countries. At the World Population Conference in Bucharest in 1974, the demographic transition theory was perhaps best expressed by the attractive sentiments "development is the best contraceptive" and "take care of the people and population will take care of itself" (Teitelbaum, 1975).

Yet the demographic transition theory has been challenged in a number of ways. Throughout most of the 1970s, a debate took place over whether socioeconomic developments were solely responsible for fertility declines. Parallel to this debate, there has been a reexamination of the demographic transition theory. Studies by the European Fertility Project under the direction of Ansley Coale reveal that the historical fertility decline in European countries occurred in a broad range of socioeconomic settings. In fact many European areas differed widely in the degree of industrialization but followed similar patterns of fertility changes (Coale, 1973, 1984; Knodel and van de Walle, 1979; van de Walle and Knodel, 1980).

The reexamination of the demographic transition theory also raises questions concerning if the theory can be applied to developing countries. In an influential article published in *Science* in 1975, Teitelbaum discussed in much detail the irrelevance of the demographic transition theory for understanding population changes in developing countries (Teitelbaum, 1975). The most obvious reason is that conditions in developing countries will never parallel to those of Europe in the 19th century in terms of either economic or social developments. Even if demographic changes do reflect trends of socioeconomic development, experiences in developing countries will differ from those of Europe, not only in timing and speed but also in characters (Findlay and Findlay, 1987; Freedman, 1979, 1986; Hess, 1988; Teitelbaum, 1975).

Another criticism lies in the complaint that the demographic transition theory is merely descriptive, thereby offering little to understand why or how socioeconomic changes have brought about fertility transitions (Handwerker, 1986). According to Davis and Blake (1956), there are some "intermediate variables" between fertility transitions and socioeconomic developments. Fertility is directly influenced by a set of "intermediate variables," and modernization, in turn, operates only indirectly on fertility through these determinants (Davis and Blake, 1956). Bongaarts (1978) further quantifies these variables and isolates the effect of each factor on fertility. In 1963 Davis proposed his theory of demographic change and response as an adjunct to the demographic transition theory. In order to examine the mechanism through which a mortality decline leads to a fertility decline, Davis focused on how people responded to demographic changes. According to Davis, with more survival of children through adulthood, there is a great pressure on family resources so that people have to reorganize their lives to relieve the pressure. In this regard people respond to the demographic change in terms of personal goals rather than national goals. Individual responses are determined by the means available to them. If there are opportunities for social and economic improvements, people will take the chances and avoid large families that may increase the pressure (Davis, 1963; Weeks, 1989).

In spite of various criticisms, the demographic transition theory is very influential in fertility studies. Other sociological perspectives, including the emphasis on social institutions or social norms can find their starting points here.

The social institutional approach attempts to work on the linkage between modernization and fertility as suggested by the demographic transition theory. With the assumption that "demographic behavior ... is governed in important respects by underlying patterns of social and administrative organization" (McNicoll, 1978: 50), the social institutional approach focuses on the institutional contexts in a society. It is postulated that, because fertility takes place in a particular institutional environment and responds to changes in that environment, institutional settings may function as immediate determinants of fertility decline (McNicoll, 1982). As Potter (1983) summarized, an institution may influence fertility

1. by changing the economic costs and benefits of children;
2. by changing internalized values concerning the family, marriage and fertility; and
3. by changing the social and administrative pressures bearing on the reproductive behavior of individuals and couples (Potter, 1983: 628).

A number of institutions have been studied with relation to fertility. They are classified into three categories: 1) institutions that determine the economic contributions that children can make, such as family and institutions providing old-age security and welfare; 2) institutions that create tastes for or against children, such as education, religion, mass media, or advertising; and 3) institutions with political power in defining population goals and mobilizing resources to meet them (Bulatao and Lee, 1982).

Among the various social institutions, family has been frequently mentioned since a family provides a structured environment in which the demand for children is formulated and realized. Studies on this aspect center on economic relationships, division of labor, and the power structure within families, represented by two influential studies: Caldwell's wealth flow theory (Caldwell, 1982a, 1982b, 1987) and Davis' study of sex roles within families (Davis, 1984).

According to Caldwell, a fundamental issue in the demographic transition

...is the *direction and magnitude of intergeneration wealth flows* or the net balance of the two flows - one from parents to children and the other from children to parents... (Caldwell, 1987: 55-56).

In traditional societies, children are a source of income and support for parents, and produce far more than what they cost. The flow of wealth is from children to parents. However, the process of modernization changes not only family structures (from large, extended families to small, nuclear families), but also family economy and relations. Children begin to cost parents more than what their parents can get from them. As the wealth flow reverses, the value of children, and thereby the demand for children, declines (Caldwell, 1982a, 1982b).

Caldwell (1982a) pays special attention to the role that education plays in changing the flow of wealth. Education facilitates the rapid spread of new ideas and information, which promotes the process of modernization; education also reduces the chance of a child working inside and outside the home, not only because of certain hours needed in school attendance, but also that the child may want to distance from the tradition of work. On the one hand, children learn a new morality from school and challenge the old morals governing traditional families. Educated parents, on the other hand, tend to recognize that demands for educated children are legitimate. In this way, both family and education, as institutional settings within which fertility decisions are made and related, alter individuals' fertility desires (Caldwell, 1982a).

The sex-role study by Davis examines the relationship between industrialization and fertility in terms of the spousal division of labor (Davis, 1984). Davis describes three different types of division of labor between a husband and a wife: 1) a household economic system that is characterized by the dominance of the husband and the fact that both the husband and the wife work; 2) a breadwinner system in which the husband is a "breadwinner" while the wife becomes a "homemaker"; and 3) an egalitarian system that is distinguished by its equalization of rights and obligations of the spouses in both workplace and the home. The first two forms are conductive to producing many children while the third form typically leads to low fertility. According to Davis, it is industrialization that changes the spousal division of labor within families from the household system to the breadwinner system, and finally to the egalitarian system. The shift results in a decline in demands for children (Davis, 1984; Davis and van den Oever, 1986).

Some other social institutions have also been investigated with respect to their influences on fertility. For instance, Adnan (1982) develops the thesis that the stratification system in a country may conserve high fertility. Based on his analyses of three broad classes in Bangladesh, Adnan (1982) implies that if a stratification system is such that there is a dominant class exercising tight control over most economic opportunities, then the dominant class will shape the fertility orientations of all classes in the society (Adnan, 1982; Namboodiri, 1986). Another example of the institutional approach is provided by a study of village and family life in Guangdong province, China, conducted by Parish and Whyte (1978). With particular reference to the Chinese land reform and agricultural collectivization, Parish and Whyte observe how the new rural economic structures and organizations can have more or less direct impact on reproductive behavior (Parish and Whyte, 1978).

In short, institutional studies emphasize such "intermediate" factors as social, economic, political, and administrative structures. It is believed that these studies provide bridges to overcome the divorce between "macro" socioeconomic development and "micro" fertility behavior (Potter, 1983).

The Normative Theory

Despite its close relation with the institutional perspective, the normative approach to the study of fertility is distinct with respect to its emphasis on the importance of social constraints on individuals' reproductive behavior. This approach assumes that, within a society, norms about family sizes are developed in response to changes in socioeconomic and demographic conditions, which, in turn, influence the reproductive behavior of the members in that society. Therefore, the concept of normative structure or norm is often used to explain, interpret, and predict variations and trends of fertility behavior and family planning (Freedman, 1963, 1975; Fried and Udry, 1980; Hawthorn, 1970; Mason, 1983; Ory, 1978; Raina, 1969; Ryder, 1980; Udry, 1982).

One of the basic arguments in this perspective is to consider social norms of fertility as a collectively rational reaction to a common problem. Freedman (1963) states that

...when many members of a society face a recurrent common problem with important social consequences they tend to develop a normative solution for it. This solution, a set of rules for behavior in a particular situation, becomes part of the culture, and the society indoctrinates its members to conform more or less closely to the norms by implicit or explicit rewards and punishments (Freedman, 1963: 222).

Like other social norms, norms about family sizes in a society are developed as a social control mechanism to achieve socially valued goals (Raina, 1969).

Another major aspect of the normative approach involves the question of how individuals' reproductive behavior can be normatively constrained (Mason, 1983). Generally speaking, family size desires can be normatively controlled by direct prescription of the number of children that a couple should bear (Mason, 1983). A society or a group imposes a set of coercive constraints upon its members in order to protect its interests. Norms about family sizes are likely to be in terms of a range in the numbers of children that are permissible and desirable. Individuals acquire these norms through a process of indoctrination. These norms are not only external rules, but also frequently internalized as part of personality. Thus a couple may choose a normatively acceptable family size over another because it would be wrong to select the other (Mason, 1983; Ory, 1978; Ryder, 1980).

Fertility behavior can also be constrained indirectly by prescriptions of such related matters as marriage, timing of intercourse, and family planning (Freedman, 1963). For example, studies show that fertility was only moderately high in many areas of pre-industrial Europe. One explanation is that the moderate level was kept by particular cultural norms such as late marriage and prolonged breastfeeding. Although these norms or customs were not directly related to the number of children already born, they were related to the number of children that couple would have (Coale, 1984; Freedman, 1963). Social norms about contraception are obviously an important area of inquiry. In addition to data from pre-industrial Europe, studies on the demographic transition in contemporary developing countries have provided further evidence in this regard. New reproductive norms, consistent with government population policies and implemented through family planning programs, have successfully altered individuals' attitudes toward birth control measures and their fertility behavior (Kaufman, 1983; Mauldin, 1982).

Furthermore, reproductive behavior by individuals may be constrained indirectly through normative pressures on particular social, economic, political obligations between parents and children, husbands and wives, or individuals and the community (Mason, 1983). Norms governing social relations and institutions may not directly affect fertility or family sizes, but they may indirectly do so. For instance, changes of obligations between parents and children, resulting from social and economic developments, may affect the value of children to parents in a given society. The decline in the value of children further decreases the demand for children and the number of children. This relationship has been revealed by a number of studies on values of children, as mentioned earlier.

Still other studies tend to observe the mechanism through which normative pressures constrain fertility behavior in terms of demographic characteristics. Some studies reveal that the impact of normative pressures on family planning and pregnancy varies with parity (Fried and Udry, 1980; Udry, 1982). In addition, a study by Clay and Zuiches (1980) uncovers the gender variation between husbands and wives with regard to their norm formations of ideal family sizes.

The normative explanation of demands for children, with its focus on social norms, customs, or cultures, should not be isolated from other sociological perspectives. On the one hand, family size norms are deeply embedded in particular social institutions in a given society; the norms, on the other hand, also change corresponding to socioeconomic and demographic developments in that society. In fact Freedman's framework emphasizes the importance of societal norms about family sizes and about the "intermediate variables" for explaining the level of fertility in a society, while taking into account the environmental, socioeconomic, and demographic structures in that society (Freedman, 1975).

EVALUATION

All theoretical schools and perspectives sketched above, while emphasizing different factors, tend to explore one, or some, aspect of fertility determinants. The enormous complexity of fertility determinants is ascribed to the intricate nature of the subject. Fertility is a complex social phenomenon. It is both a biological behavior with physiological constraints and a social behavior that attaches to its socioeconomic and cultural settings. The demand for children by couples may exhibit both particular attributes within families and collective properties in a given society. Having children or not may be the result of a couple's free decision, and may be caused by societal pressures. Given these complicated features, the theoretical perspectives mentioned earlier are complementary rather than substitutive to each other.

Indeed, different perspectives have made their distinct contributions to the understanding of human fertility and demands for children. My intent here, however, is not to provide an extensive evaluation on this broad regard. Instead, the focus will be their relevance to the central issue of this study - deviant fertility.

In light of the present concern, the normative perspective proposed by sociologists appears most relevant. With the assumption that a society or a group regulates reproductive behavior by norms, the normative approach tends to explain fertility behavior in a given society in terms of group survival and societal interests. Thus, fertility behavior, either normal or deviant, can be understood not merely as free choice by an individual but as results of social control, socialization, and normative constraints. In order to understand the violations of reproductive norms in a society, it is logical to ask "Why does a society develop relevant norms for regulating its members' fertility intentions and behavior?" and "How do these normative constraints operate?" Having answered the questions, the normative perspective demonstrates its main virtue.

Normative influences on fertility are dependent of social institutions. According to the institutional perspective, various institutions in a society constitute the social contexts in which reproductive norms are formulated and implemented. With regard to the formation of reproductive norms, family orientation and family planning programs are especially crucial. Furthermore, the indoctrination of a new social norm about family sizes is often accompanied by changing old institutions or by establishing new organizations. The institutional approach has provided detailed analyses to explicate how institutional changes, such as changes in family structure, improvements in education, reorganizations of economic systems, and establishment of family planning organizations, lead to declines in fertility and in the demand for children. In this way the institutional approach has contributed considerably.

The demographic transition theory, including its modified forms, is by no means able to specify all relevant determinants related to fertility decline, nor can it be used directly to predict individual fertility behavior. The theory, however, does guide us to look at broad social contexts and to examine fertility patterns in terms of reproductive responses to large-scale social and economic developments. In spite of various critics, studies have continued to show evidence of the relationship between socioeconomic conditions and fertility, at both societal and individual levels. Yet, it may be true that the relationship is neither as simple as expected, nor as direct as anticipated. The search for "intermediate" factors becomes necessary and important.

Overall, the sociological studies have indeed identified some structural factors that are relevant for understanding deviant fertility. Nevertheless, their most valuable recommendation to the present study is to examine fertility behavior of individuals in its social and institutional context. For sociologists, reproductive behavior does not occur in a vacuum but in a social setting. To fully understand this behavior, one has to take its social configurations into account.

It is often the case that the strength of one perspective is also its weakness as well. A framework that is broad, or macro, enough to encompass all the structural factors on fertility necessarily loses specificities in the micro process. This happens with sociological studies of fertility. It may be true that individuals are not free agents and their behaviors are determined by their socialization and social constraints; it is also factual that individuals are not mere cogs in a machine and that they make decisions based on their interpretations of the environmental conditions. Even under societal constraints, individuals still can adjust their fertility behavior in order to maximize their interests. However, many sociologists do not explicate the interpersonal process of fertility decision making and behavior. As a result, it is impossible to explain why people under the same social controls and constraints, in fact, behave differently. What is neglected in the sociological studies, however, becomes a focus in the psychological and economic perspectives on fertility.

The major contribution of the psychological perspective consists in its exploration of individual behavioral tendencies on which fertility behavior largely depends. Although individuals live in the same social environments, they may demonstrate different fertility motives and behavior. The psychological approach of fertility establishes a linkage between the makeup of individuals and their environments, and interprets the demand for children as an interactive product of personal dispositions and situational properties. In this way psychologists shift the attention from the societal level to the individual level, examining individual motivations, attitudes and preferences in predicting fertility behavior. In the present study, with the assumption that individuals' behavior, including both normal and deviant, is guided by their motives, intentions, and attitudes, the psychological approach will retain its important position.

With a similar micro orientation, the economic perspective holds that individuals as consumers are rational in their decision-making and will allocate their limited resources in ways that maximize total satisfaction. The most valuable endowment from this perspective is to examine the demand for children with relation to the demand of other items. In many parts of the world, especially in developing countries, parents still find children an important source of wealth, prestige, and security. However, social and economic developments are accompanied by changes not only in the rewards from children but also the rewards deriving from other opportunities. The economic approach will be useful to examine fertility decision making and behavior in terms of individual calculus of cost and benefits from fertility.

Ideally, fertility behavior, either normal or deviant, should be examined within a single framework that accounts for the determinants at both the societal and individual levels. However, the existing literature does show the potential for studying fertility determination by bringing different perspectives together.

Yet another problem remains. To what extent can the previous studies in fertility and the demand for children be applied to study "deviant" fertility in China? Previous researchers have revealed various determinants, but they inspect fertility in a similar fashion. Fertility has been observed either quantitatively or demographically. In the former, the number of children is examined, while, in the latter, the parity and sex of the births are highlighted. However, "deviant" fertility is not a simple matter of a quantitative increase in birth. The demand for children, even very strong, does not necessarily lead to the violation of productive norms. Individual couples who desire more children may tend to conform to nationally valued standards of a small family. The reasons for having children are not sufficient, although related, to explain fertility in a "deviant" manner. In short, fertility can be divided into two kinds: normal and deviant. The former refers to those within socially approved ranges, while the later involves those in opposition to socially valued expectations. This distinction has been overlooked in previous fertility studies, but it appears very significant in the present project. A new dimension and a different theoretical framework thus are needed.

CHAPTER III

THEORETICAL FORMATION

TOWARD A "DEVIANT" FERTILITY APPROACH

More than thirty years ago, Kingsley Davis (1959) called for a marriage between sociology and demography. For instance, an interest in fertility might be combined with an interest in family structure and a focus in internal migration with a concern with urbanization. It appears that integration of elements from different fields has been going forward with some hesitation and difficulty. The mutual value for the integrated disciplines is undeniably great (Davis, 1959).

Is it possible, then, to develop an approach that bridges the sociology of fertility and the sociology of deviance? In a simplified expression, the sociology of deviance attempts to offer explanations for behavior that violate social norms, while the sociology of fertility aims to explore determinants of human fertility. Despite diversities, however, there are some reasons for pursuing integration. First, there are fertility behaviors that violate dominant reproductive norms. Like other social phenomena, this occurrence deserves a sociological explanation. Second, the causes of "deviant" fertility are assumed to be multiple. With both fertility and deviance as foci in this study, the subject matter goes beyond the scope of previous sociological perspectives on fertility and classic theories of deviant behavior. Third, according to the multiple-cause assumption, one particular kind of behavior outcome such as "deviant" fertility may result from more than one set of conditions. For instance, as mentioned earlier, the determinants of demands for children are necessary but not sufficient to understand "deviant" fertility. Some other mechanisms identified by deviant behavior theories may be relevant. It is anticipated, therefore, that a new approach combining both fields will provide a better explanation in this regard.

The next question is how to link the two different perspectives together. The synthesis can be either a "mixed" model or an "integrated" one. The distinction is applicable to the present research. A "mixed" model can be developed by simply combining variables identified by two domains, with little regard for the conceptualization of variables in terms of logical reconciliation. An "integrated" model indeed is more desirable for this study, which attempts to reconcile differences in the assumptions and propositions from sociology of fertility and sociology of deviance. It will also provide explanations of how these combined factors are related to each other in a coherent theoretical perspective. This is the "deviant" fertility approach that is to be used for the present research.

CONCEPTS

Norms, Normative Constraint, Conflicts, and Deviation

Considering the importance of the concept of "norm" to sociology, it is surprising just how little agreement exists on the definition of norms, much less on the processes through which norms constrain individual behavior (Cancian, 1975; Mason, 1983). In an article published in *American Journal of Sociology* in 1965, Jack Gibbs listed seven different definitions of "norm" (Gibbs, 1965). After a quarter of a century, the number may be doubled, if not tripled. In spite of this variance, however, certain assumptions about the nature of norms are shared by most sociologists. Briefly, first, a social norm is a collective evaluation of behavior with respect to what it ought to be; second, a social norm constitutes a collective expectation in terms of what behavior will be; third, a social norm provides most individuals with incentives to behave in ways they would not otherwise behave; fourth, a social norm involves particular reactions to behavior, including applying sanctions (Blake and Davis, 1964; Bryant, 1990; Gibbs, 1965; Mason, 1983). Based on these assumptions, the concept of norms has often been used by sociologists to explain why people think or behave as they do under given circumstances.

No one would doubt that norms can exercise certain influence on behavior, but the question of what makes norms effective is debatable. In theory, two channels can be identified: internal constraints and external constraints. On the one hand, norms are societal or group characteristics imposed upon individuals during socialization and reinforced by social controls. On the other hand, norms can be internalized by individuals, since it is individuals who decide to behave in particular ways. In reality, norms are simultaneously both internal characteristics of individuals and external constraints imposed by the group or society.

Here the most influential perspective was put forward by Parsons (1951). He argued that most individuals have a commitment to behave as the norms of their group say they should. This commitment to norms is made during the process of socialization. In this way norms are lodged within individuals and guide their behavior as blueprints guide the behavior of a builder (Mason, 1983; Parsons, 1951). However, this blueprint theory is not free of problems. Societies, as we know them, are not only dynamic but also diverse, filled with conflicting interests and competing values. Norm conflict often results in norm violations, since fulfilling the norms of one group may violate the norms of another.

Among others, the cultural conflict theory of deviance is particularly relevant here. In his pamphlet *Cultural Conflict and Crime*, Thorsten Sellin (1938) maintained that human beings are born into cultures that provide meanings to behavior and that behavior is normatively oriented. People act in accordance with the rules of the groups in which they are members. However, as a society becomes more and more complex, individuals are exposed to many different sets of conduct norms and values, and their behaviors are governed by conflicting norms. In Sellin's own words:

> The more complex a culture becomes, the more likely it is that the number of normative groups which affect a person will be large, and the greater is the chance that the norms of these groups will fail to agree, no matter how much they may overlap as a result of a common acceptance of certain norms (Sellin, 1938: 29).

In this situation, therefore, individuals who take certain kinds of normative actions may deviate from the standpoint of other groups. According to Sellin (1938), these processes can account for much of the deviant behavior by the foreign-born in the United States. Since he devoted much of his attention to cultural conflicts among immigrants from different cultural backgrounds, Sellin spent little time depicting details about other aspects of cultural conflicts (McCaghy, 1985).

Cultural conflicts are not necessarily limited to the diversity of normative traditions brought by different ethnic groups. Cultural conflicts of conduct norms may exist within a single ethnic group. Modern societies are active and dynamic. Rapid social and economic changes are associated with transformations in attitudes, values, and norms. Some behavior, such as cigarette smoking, that was considered as normal years ago, is regarded as deviant today (Bryant, 1990). As long as norms change, what constitutes a deviant act is not constant.

Facing normative changes, individuals may find themselves with a dilemma. On the one hand, they may continue to behave as they used to, regardless of reactions from others. On the other hand, they may deviate from their groups and modify their behavior in order to be accepted by others in the society.

Furthermore, conflicts may also involve a process of decision making. This argument seems debatable. According to the Parsonsian and some other approaches, individuals respond to norms unconsciously because norms are internalized (Mason, 1983). If so, a calculated decision-making process is out of the question. However, this idealized situation may not fit the fact of norm conflicts. Presumably, if individuals can perceive conflicts and know their relevant consequences (punishments or rewards), it sounds logical to posit a conscious calculation on the costs and the benefits of conformity versus deviance.

Reproductive Norms, Pressures, Conflicts and Fertility Deviation

Reproductive norms here refer to those that explicitly govern family sizes. Such family size norms are expressed in terms of a range in number of children that are optimum or desirable. In other words, reproductive norms define how many children that married couples ought to have. The norms are developed as a means for regulating reproductive behavior in a given society. Different societies or groups establish different reproductive norms according their own interests and problems. The norm for a particular culture or group may be "two or three children," while the norm of "as many as possible" may be prevalent in other societies.

Normative pressures with regard to family sizes, like other norms, influence reproductive behavior in many different ways. One mechanism identified is an early internalization of family size norms. Many youngsters begin to formulate thoughts on how many children they would like to have for themselves (Westoff and Potvin, 1966). The demographic structure of a family conditions its norms, which are accepted by its children and further influence their own family sizes (Gustavus, 1973; Gustavus and Nam, 1970; Hendershot, 1969). Accordingly, the family of origin acts as one mechanism for transmitting family size norms from one generation to another. In addition, normative pressures also come from intimate groups of individuals, including friends, relatives, and spouses. Given that the topic of family sizes is generally of a confidential nature in the United States, norm enforcement is likely to occur within intimate groupings (Clay and Zuiches, 1980).

Official normative pressures are often imposed on individuals through family planning programs. The main focus of family planning programs in many developing countries is to establish a norm of small families and to bring about behavioral changes to reduce fertility. It is evident that, under the pressure of these programs, many married couples in these countries are planning their families in accordance with the national valued goals. China is considered one of the success stories in this regard (Kaufman, 1983; Mauldin, 1982).

Normative change is gradual rather than sudden. A new official norm about family sizes may be established by a government to alter individual fertility desires and behavior. At the same time, traditional or old reproductive norms may continue to govern individual fertility intentions and actions. As a result, the new norm of small family sizes may exist side by side with the traditional large family ideal. The modern norm of small family sizes conflicts with the traditional ideal, but they exist simultaneously and jointly determine people's fertility desires and behavior. At least three reasons can be found for this coexistence. First, the transformation of norms should be accompanied with appropriate institutional changes. Institutional changes, however, may not be available in some cases. Second, norms regarding family sizes are related to norms governing other aspects of individual behavior. It is unrealistic to expect a change of family size norms alone. Third, traditional norms of family sizes are rooted so deeply in cultural heritage and have such powerful sanctions that old behavior patterns tend to continue, even during the process of social change.

The conflict between traditional and modern norms regarding family sizes creates a state of ambivalence. Under this circumstance, individual couples may conform to the new small family norm even though they may not be completely convinced, or they may adhere to the heritage of a large family. Considering the costs and benefits of the alternatives, many couples make their choices rationally. Their demographic characteristics, especially educational attainment and age, influence the choices. In any case, if a married couple has a greater number of children than the number that is officially valued, they violate present state-established family size norms; their reproductive behavior is considered deviant. In this strict usage, *deviant fertility refers to the reproductive behavior that violates dominant family size norms by having more than the accepted number of children.*

DEVIANT FERTILITY IN CHINA

Deviant fertility, like other deviant behavior, does not occur in a social vacuum but in certain social contexts and conditions. Thus, a better understanding of deviant fertility in China must include an appreciation of Chinese culture and tradition, political systems, and social conditions. The establishment of current reproductive norms, the conflicts between the state-established family planning norms and traditional large-family norms, and the violations of the current official family planning norms all have their foundations in the structure and organization of social institutions in China.

Family Planning Policies and Reproductive Norms

The current reproductive norms in China are developed by government-sponsored family planning programs. In the process of the demographic transition experienced by many developed and developing countries, small family size norms have been externally introduced and dispersed through either a spontaneous process of diffusion without the support of institutional agencies or a deliberate process enforced by governments and social institutions. While many developed countries experienced the former process in their demographic transition, most developing nations today are experiencing the later. In spite of the influence of Western ideas regarding family sizes through education and mass media, the development of current reproductive norms in China largely results from efforts by family planning programs (Knodel and van de Walle, 1979; Mauldin, 1982; Wang, 1990).

Since the establishment of the communist government in 1949, there have been four family planing campaigns: The First Campaign, 1956-1958, The Second Campaign, 1962-1966, The Later-Longer-Fewer Campaign, 1971-1979, and The One-Child Campaign, 1979-present. However, the last two programs are much more effective and well documented (Banister, 1987; Chen and Kols, 1982; Congress of the United States, 1982; Croll, Davin, and Kane, 1985; Kane, 1987; Platte, 1984; Tien, 1980, 1983; Yu, 1979).

In 1971, the Chinese government launched its third campaign, the so-called Later-Longer-Fewer campaign. Married couples were required to obey three reproductive norms: to marry later (wan), to extend the interval between births (xi), and to have fewer children (shao). In rural areas men were encouraged to postpone marriage until 25 and women until 23; and in cities they were encouraged to postpone marriage for additional two years. The government urged that births should be spaced three or four years apart. Urban couples should limit themselves to having two children and rural couples to three. Although the Later-Longer-Fewer campaign was notably successful in reducing fertility rates, the Chinese leadership in 1979 decided to achieve further decrease of fertility in order to reach the goal of "Four Modernizations."[3] Thus China's fourth family planning campaign, known as the One-Child Campaign, was initiated. In 1980 the goals of the campaign were stated in quantitative terms,

> ...that 95 percent of married couples in the cities and 90 percent in the countryside will have only one child in due course, so that the total population of China will be controlled at about 1.2 billion by the end of the century (Chen, 1980).

The family planning policies in China are implemented in a highly organized social structure with strong ideological controls. The Chinese political system can effectively transmit and enforce the family planning policies of the central government to lower levels. Local grassroots units, such as residence committees in cities and communes and production brigades in rural areas, carry the policies to every individual. The Communist Party, existing in every large and small organization within the country, acts as the leader in implementation of the family planning policies. In addition, many civic associations such as the women's federations and trade unions are supplementary to the formal governmental apparatus for the policy implementation. The network of the family planning program is complex but well organized. This system makes it possible for family planning policies and new ideas about small family sizes to reach and influence every family and its members.

---

[3] The modernization of agriculture, industry, defense, and science/technology.

In addition to providing birth control information and services, Chinese family planning programs aim to introduce and enforce new reproductive norms through various channels. Slogans, posters, mass media, speeches, and public exhibits all carry family planning messages. Songs and plays are used for propagating new family planning norms. The benefits and importance of planned childbirth are discussed in numerous study group meetings for men and women. Those who fail to attend study group meetings are visited by family planning officers in their homes. These persuasive efforts are very effective in introducing new norms of fertility and mobilizing married couples to conform to the new reproductive norms.

Constraints of New Reproductive Norms

To better understand the normative constraints of fertility in China, one has to examine a bigger picture - normative structures in China. Under a totalitarian regime, Chinese people have been accustomed to following what the government wants them to do. This general behavior pattern is the key to understand normative constraints in general and the constraints of reproductive behavior in particular in China. Here, the official ideology and social controls in terms of rewards and punishments deserve consideration.

According to the official ideology in China, the government by definition represents the interests of the people. Thus, whatever the government appeals to are always for the benefit of the people and the society. Individuals are required to be loyal to the government and to sacrifice their own interests for social obligations (Wilson, 1981). This "collectivism" or "state loyalty" becomes a normative pattern of thinking, feeling, and acting of ordinary Chinese citizens. This behavior pattern effectively facilitates the implementation of government projects, including family planning programs.

Chinese family planning campaigns have always relied heavily upon ideological efforts to gain acceptance of the new fertility norms. In doing so, the interests of an individual are often linked with those of the state and society. It has been emphasized by the government that family planning and population growth controls are not only for the well-being of individuals and their families, but more importantly for the prosperity of the nation and the happiness of generations to come (Liang, 1989; Wasserstrom, 1987). In implementing the one-child policy, the Chinese government is aware of the sacrifice it demands of the young generation (Croll, 1985). However, the policy states that individuals ought to accept the new norms and limit their family sizes for the long-term interests of the nation and whole society, even if it directly counters their own family benefits. Muhua Chen, Vice Premier and Director of the State Council Birth Planning Leading Group, asserts it clearly:

> To the extent that the interests of individuals come into conflict with those of the state and the collective, the former should voluntarily be subordinated to the latter (Chen, 1981: 76).

Given the general behavior pattern of obeying government commands and its implications in family planning campaigns, it is not surprising that some people, especially those who are in leadership positions and those with strong political orientations, voluntarily and consciously take the government requests as their rules for behavior.

The majority are also coerced into following the government's family planning policies. For these people, rewards and punishments are often calculated. In China, the government controls most social resources and thereby many aspects of an individual's life. It is easy for the government to apply sanctions on individual behavior. Rewards and punishments are often well defined.

In the case of family planning, economic incentives and constraints constitute a part of the campaign. For example, for an urban family with a one-child certificate, parents receive a monthly stipend (about 5 to 8 percent of the average worker's wage) until the child reaches age 14. The couple will also be entitled to have housing space equally to that given to a two-child family. Their child will be given priority in admission to nurseries, kindergartens, school programs, and even in job assignments. However, if a couple breaks their pledges by having two or more children, they have to pay for hospital costs, medical care, and grain rations of the extra children. Their monthly wages may be reduced by 10 percent or more, and they may be ineligible for job promotions for three years (Chen and Kols, 1982; David, 1982; Kane, 1985;

Ma, 1989). A one-child couple residing in a rural area is supposed to receive additional monthly work points each year until the child reaches age 14, an adult grain ration for the child, and a private plot of land the same size as other families with more children. In rural areas, penalties for having children outside the plan include withholding grain allocations and charging for school and medical care. In addition, their work points are reduced for all the years when the out-of-plan children are growing up (Banister, 1984; David, 1982; Davin, 1985).

In short, the Chinese family planning programs are both voluntary and coercive in nature. On the one hand, ideological education functions to persuade individual couples to conform to the new fertility norms. On the other hand, the economic and administrative incentives for one-child families and penalties for out-of-plan births push married couples toward conforming to the new family planning norms. The normative constraints from these two channels are particularly relevant to the implementation of the family planning policies. The Chinese experience of establishing new norms of fertility behavior, as Croll (1985, p. 32) states, "reflects the quite central belief in China that ideology and organization can introduce and maintain momentum in social change."

Fertility Norm Violations in China

In spite of the success of the Chinese family planning programs, fertility behavior that violates the planning regulations and norms still exists. Its quantitative dimension can be reported by the census and other surveys. It is also important, however, to explore the qualitative components of the known acts. Five examples of fertility deviance are described below.

Case one. A "rich" farmer couple of Gansu province had two daughters but insisted on having a third child. It was a boy. Although they had to pay ¥2,000 (about 25% of their annual income), they were very happy and named their newborn son "bugui" - meaning inexpensive (Feng, 1989).

Case two. A party cadre of a village in Shanxi province used his power to obtain "defect" certificates for his newborn infants who were not physically defective in any way. Eventually, he had eight children without any penalty (Mo, 1990).

Case three. A farmer of Guangdong province received a one-child certificate after the birth of his first child, a girl. However, he reported that the girl died and his wife had a boy the next year. The "dead" girl then returned home from her aunt's residence in another village (World Journal, 1991).

Case four. An "unplanned birth" village was formed in the Xinjiang autonomous region. All residents were temporary and came from different parts of the country, but they had the common goal: to escape from family planning. Living in poor conditions and having an average of two to five children, they vowed not to go home until they had a son (Mo, 1990).

Case five. A farmer and his wife had two daughters and wanted to have a son. In order to avoid local family planning personnel, he built a narrow space between two walls to hide his wife. After seven years of physical and mental torment, his wife finally gave birth to a son. The tragic result was that, due to the inhuman living condition, the mother became paralytic and the infant suffered from serious diseases (World Journal, 1992).

These selected cases by no means represent all instances of fertility deviance in China, but they do illustrate some characteristics of the phenomenon. First, deviant fertility is closely related to son preference. Many couples have "deviant" births because they only have female offspring. Second, those couples may employ deviant means to reach their desires for a male child. They use money or power, and they hide or run away in order to escape punishment for their behavior. Third, fertility deviance occurs with greater frequency in rural areas than in urban regions. Rural farmers are more likely to benefit from their children and are less controlled by the government. Finally, Chinese women are participants in and victims of deviant fertility. Actors involved in fertility deviance include both husbands and wives. Yet Chinese women, including those unwanted baby girls and their mothers, suffer more than their male counterparts.

In short, deviant fertility in China is a complex social phenomenon, a reflection of both Chinese traditions and current social structures. Strong messages from the current family planning programs have successfully reached individual families and created conflicts with the traditional constraints of

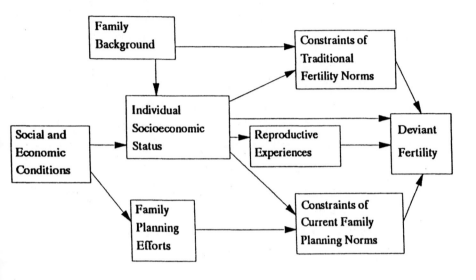

Figure 3.1 Diagram of Theoretical Model Predicting Deviant Fertility

fertility behavior. These conflicts are the keys to understanding deviant fertility in China.

MODEL SPECIFICATION AND HYPOTHESES

Based on the concepts discussed above and the relevant previous studies summarized, a theoretical model is presented in Figure 3.1. A fundamental assumption underlying the model is that deviant fertility is the product of normative conflicts between pressures from traditional reproductive norms and constraints of current family planning policy norms. It is also assumed that the degrees of constraints by the traditional and the current fertility norms depend on a wide range of factors. These factors are expected to exist at societal, family, and individual levels, such as family backgrounds, family relations, previous reproductive experiences, socioeconomic development, and family planning efforts. Moreover, the influences of socioeconomic development, family backgrounds, family relations, family planning efforts, and individual reproductive experiences of deviant fertility are assumed to be indirect through the normative constraints. On the ground of these relationships, several hypotheses are generated.

Constraints of Traditional Fertility Norms. The model assumes a direct link between deviant fertility and traditional norm constraints. This relationship is derived from the cultural conflict perspective of deviance. It is speculated that, on the one hand, deviant fertility in China is immediately determined by the extent to which individual couples are constrained by traditional fertility norms. On the other hand, influences of traditional norms are affected directly by family backgrounds, socioeconomic characteristics, family relations, and reproductive experiences and indirectly by social and economic conditions.

Hypothesis 1: Chinese couples who have strong traditional norm constraints of fertility are more likely to have deviant fertility than those couples who do not have strong traditional pressures.

Constraints of Current Family Planning Norms. The assumption that normative conflicts lead to deviant fertility underlies the causal relations between deviant fertility and constraints of current family planning norms. Different from traditional norm pressures, the degree of the constraints largely depends on family planning efforts. In addition, individual socioeconomic characteristics and reproductive experiences are also directly related to the extent to which individuals are compelled by family planning restrictions.

Hypothesis 2: Chinese couples who are constrained by new family planning norms are less likely to have deviant fertility than those couples who are not significantly limited by the new fertility norms.

Individual Reproductive Experiences. Individual reproductive experiences refer particularly to previous births in terms of sex, infant survival, and pregnancy experiences. These experiences are believed to influence fertility attitudes and behavior. It is also assumed that reproductive experiences are not only the product of individuals' biological factors, but also the outcome of their social and economic status. It is particularly true with respect to infant care and survival. Those couples with high educational attainment and income may provide more appropriate infant care. Moreover, given that the tradition of son preference is prevalent and strong, it is likely that couples who have only female offspring want to have more, even at the cost of violating current reproductive norms.

Hypothesis 3: Chinese couples who have unfortunate reproductive experiences are more likely to be involved with deviant fertility than those who do not have such experience.

Hypothesis 4: Chinese couples who have only female children are more likely to commit fertility deviance than those couples who have previous male offspring.

Family Relations. Family relations mainly refer to relationships between a married couple and their parents. Specifically, whether or not a married couple is living with their parents after their marriage and how frequently they visit their parents if they do not live together are related to the influence of the traditional norms. The assumption here is that older generations are more likely to be concerned about carrying on family lines and firmly hold traditional fertility ideals. Living in an extended family, therefore, tends to encourage the impact of traditional fertility norms on the married couple, and then leads to the violation of current fertility regulations.

Hypothesis 5: Chinese couples who live with their parents, especially parents on the husband's side, are more likely to have deviant fertility than others.

Individual Socioeconomic Characteristics. Individual social and economic attributes, especially educational attainments, occupational status, and family income, are assumed to be the crucial factors related to deviant fertility. Also, individual socioeconomic status may affect the magnitude of normative pressures from both traditional and current family planning directions. Among the socioeconomic characteristics, place of residence is also an important factor. Whether individual couples who live in rural or urban areas determines their lifestyles and opportunities, which will influence the degree of exposure to modern ideas and of the control imposed by the government. Moreover, the proposed model also depicts two additional links in which individuals' socioeconomic features are influenced by large-scale social conditions and their family backgrounds.

Hypothesis 6: Chinese couples who enjoy higher socioeconomic status are more likely to be constrained by current family planning norms than those couples with lower socioeconomic status.

Hypothesis 7: Chinese couples who reside in rural areas are more likely than those living in cities to accept traditional fertility ideals and commit fertility deviance.

Family Backgrounds. Family backgrounds such as the educational level of parents are used as a proxy to measure family influences on fertility ideals held by individuals. Based on the assumption that fertility norms may be transmitted from one generation to another, family backgrounds are assumed to influence the degree of constraints from traditional norms about family sizes. This influence may, in turn, lead to deviant fertility outcomes.

Hypothesis 8: Chinese couples who grew up in families with low socioeconomic status are more likely to be influenced by traditional family ideals than those who came from better-off families.

Family Planning Efforts. Family planning efforts are assumed to impose normative controls directly on individual couples. This relation in fact reflects a major objective of the family planning program in China. Constraints of family planning deter fertility norm violations in China. The family planning efforts, however, are conditioned upon macro-level social and economic conditions.

Hypothesis 9: Chinese couples who are personally contacted by family planning personnel are more likely to follow the new reproductive regulations than those couples who are not strongly approached by family planning programs.

Social and Economic Conditions. Identified by many studies following the demographic transition perspective, social and economic developments serve as background factors in the proposed model. Social and economic conditions at a macro level are supposed to influence family planning efforts in a given community. The model also assumes a direct link between macro-level socioeconomic developments and individual social and economic characteristics.

CHAPTER IV

METHODOLOGY

DATA SOURCES

This study uses data from five different sources, which are listed as follows:

1) In-Depth Fertility Survey, Guangdong;
2) Old-Age Security Survey, Panyu county, Guangdong;
3) Official Records of Panyu Family Planning Commission, 1988-1990;
4) Supplementary Data on Family Planning Efforts, 1987;
5) Supplementary Data From the Third Population Census of China, 1982.

In-Depth Fertility Survey (IDFS)

The In-Depth Fertility Survey was the first probability sampling survey on detailed fertility information ever done in China (Guo, 1990). The survey was conducted by the State Statistical Bureau and the related statistical bureaus in several provinces and municipalities of China. The main purpose of the survey, as stated by the designers and organizers, was to get knowledge of the fertility level and trend of the Chinese population, analyze the factors determining women's fertility, learn the advanced experiences of WFS to improve the capability in research of fertility and demographic aspects, and provide rich scientific data for the formulation of the country's population policy (China's State Statistical Bureau, 1987: 1).

The survey was divided into two phases. The first phase began in April 1985 in two provinces and one municipality: Hebei, Shanxi, and Shanghai. The second phase was carried out two years later in Beijing, Liaoning, Shangdong, Guangdong, Guizhou, and Gansu. The survey was administered by personal interviews and conducted at three different levels: community, household, and individual women.[4] Household-level data, with 28 variables, were collected among population residing in each selected household and the household members' demographic characteristics such as age, sex, marital status, and some economic indicators. In these households, ever-married women aged under 50 were eligible for detailed personal interviews. Questionnaires with more than 100 items were used to gather detailed information about eligible women's backgrounds, marriage and pregnancy histories, child care, knowledge and uses of contraception, fertility preferences, and other factors related to fertility (China's State Statistical Bureau, 1987).

The dataset used in this study, the In-Depth Fertility Survey of Guangdong, was a part of the nationwide survey. A mixture of stratified, multistage, systematic, and proportional probability sampling techniques was applied to identify a representative sample. Consequently, seven cities and 30 counties in Guangdong were selected. The survey eventually investigated 989 households with information on 42,510 household members and interviewed 6,654 ever-married women aged 49 or younger.

---

[4] The community-level data are not available for this present study.

Old-Age Security Survey (OASS)

The Old-Age Security Survey was conducted by the Department of Social Problems, Academy of Social Science in Guangzhou, China. The survey, March 1987 through April 1988, was carried out within one county of Guangdong - Panyu. Four "xiang"[5] were randomly selected. Within each "xiang," four productive teams were further chosen. Finally, within each productive team, 26 households were selected. This resulted in a total of 416 rural households. Of the selected households, 231 were eligible with the presence of both a husband and a wife (He, Kuang and Lu, 1987).

The survey was originally designed to examine rural couples' old-age security concerns and was administered by personal interviews with questionnaires. The questionnaires were divided into husband forms and wife forms, including about 300 questions on marriage and fertility, family backgrounds, relations with parents, current family structures, expectations for children, and economic and living conditions. Of the 231 selected households, some 220 completed both the husband and wife questionnaires, resulting in a 95% response rate (Department of Social Problems, 1988).

Records of the County Family Planning Commission (RCFPC)

The documents were obtained by the author for the present study, with the help of the Academy of Social Sciences in Guangzhou, China. Panyu county was selected because of the availability of data and the research site identical with the old-age security survey. Within the Chinese political system, the family planning commission in each county or city is responsible for reporting its family planning situations to the provincial commission. The formal written reports, annually or semiannually, usually come with relevant statistical data that provide overall family planning information. Annual statistical reports of 1988 and 1989 and the semiannual one of 1990 from the family planning commission of Panyu County were used in this study.

The unit of the family planning records was "xiang." There were 24 units in the Panyu family planning reports. The reports contained 35 items, including

---

[5]"Xiang" or township is a rural administrative unit under the county.

birth control operations (abortion, sterilization, and IUD), unplanned pregnancies, unplanned births, family planning rates,[6] and information about population growth and marriage.

Supplementary Data

There were two supplementary data sources, one describing socioeconomic conditions and the other about family planning efforts. Both data assortments were corresponding to the counties and cities included in the In-Depth Fertility Survey. The supplementary data were merged into the fertility data set.

The list of selected counties and cities in the fertility survey was obtained from China Statistical Information & Consultancy Service Center in March 1991. According to identified counties and cities, sociologists at the Academy of Social Science in Guangzhou called the family planning commission in each selected county or city and required them to provide information about monetary expenses of family planning in 1987 and the amount per capita. The data collection was finished in May 1991.

Another source of the supplementary data came from published results of the 1982 Third Population Census of China. The data included county- or city-level information about population distribution, industrialization, and educational achievements (Population Census Office, 1987). The variables were used to measure macro-level social and economic conditions of selected counties and cities included in the fertility survey.

DATA ASSESSMENTS

Data used in this study are secondary, supplemented by primary analysis of RCFPC data. Since deviant fertility is a new topic of inquiry, little effort has been made in this direction, not to mention existing data sets on this focus. Given this situation, it becomes important to admit the difficulty of hypothesis tests, to discuss the possible biases, and to suggest specific ways for further

---

[6] Family planning rates are calculated, by family planning personnel, based on the following formula:
FPR =[(first birth-premarital birth+planned second births)/(total births)]*100.

studies. In this way, the secondary data, with their strengths and weaknesses, can be used scientifically and honestly.

The In-Depth Fertility Survey was developed on the basis of experiences of the World Fertility Survey (WFS) in many developing countries. The survey enriches fertility knowledge by providing information on histories of marriage, pregnancy, and contraceptive practices as well as reproductive experiences. In addition, the survey includes questions about individual socioeconomic characteristics and fertility desires and preferences. Thus, in combining with some macro-level indicators, the survey data can be used to test most relationships identified in the theoretical model in a proximate fashion. In addition to its rich information on fertility, the data set also has the advantage of a large sample size. The sample size is particularly important for this study because it enables us to break the sample into various subgroups. The major limitation, however, is that the data are thin on information about the size of family of origin and expectations for children.

The Old-Age Security Survey has two desirable features. The first is that both husbands and wives in the selected families are included. This feature makes the data set particularly valuable because husbands and wives can be examined separately to reveal possible gender differences. For example, their family origins and their relationships with their own parents can be inspected separately, and related to their current family sizes. The second desirable feature of this survey lies in its inquiries into both husbands' and wives' perceptions of children's responsibilities to parents and parents' expectations from their children. These variables are critical for revealing the traditional ideal of family sizes and demands for children. The major disadvantage of the survey for the present study is its lack of information about family planning and previous reproductive experiences. In addition, the sample was drawn from only one county in Guangdong and the sample size is relatively small.

The family planning records of Panyu County provide an opportunity to examine the prevalence of unplanned fertility and pregnancy, according to the official accounts. Since these family planning data are over three successive years, it becomes possible to inspect trends and patterns of unplanned fertility and birth control measures in a dynamic fashion. The data, however, have to be used with caution. The reliability of the data is a major concern. First, the family planning records include only cases reported to, or known by, family planning personnel. In fact, many instances are not reported and therefore not included in the official records. Furthermore, local family planning agencies may conceal unplanned fertility cases in order to impress authorities with their "achievements." In either case, deviant fertility cases tend to be underestimated. Accordingly, there is little doubt that the data are biased toward "good news" for family planning agencies.

Each data set has its desirable and undesirable traits related to the present research focus. Given that these data sets have their distinct samples and units of analysis, it is impossible to combine them into a single format. The current study will deploy a range of data sources, each of which is used individually with specific focuses. The In-Depth Fertility Survey is used to provide an overall picture of predicting deviant fertility. The Old-Age Security Survey is employed to detect in detail how married couples' families of origin, family relations and expectations for children influence their family sizes. The record of family planning agencies is used to examine patterns and trends of deviant fertility longitudinally. Combining results from these different data sources will enrich our knowledge of deviant fertility in China from different angles.

SAMPLE DESCRIPTION

Sample Description of IDFS Data

As indicated earlier, the IDFS sample included 6,654 never-married Chinese women aged 49 or younger. The demographic profile of these women is shown in Table 4.1. Slightly more than one-third of the respondents were aged under 30 and about 42 percent were in their 30s. Approximately one in four respondents was 40 to 49 years old. The median age of the sample was 33.6.

Table 4.1

Sample Descriptions on Demographic Characteristics, IDFS Data

Demographic Characteristics	Number	Percentage
Age		
17 to 29 years old	2235	33.6
30 to 39 years old	2778	41.7
40 to 49 years old	1641	24.7
Education		
No schooling	1511	22.7
1 to 6 years	3180	47.8
7 to 12 years	1898	28.5
13 or more years	65	1.0
Husband's Education		
No schooling	296	4.5
1 to 6 years	2790	42.6
7 to 12 years	3285	50.1
13 or more years	182	2.8
Residence		
Rural	5238	78.7
Urban	1416	21.3
Nationality		
Han (majority)	6018	97.5
Other (minority)	154	2.5
Occupation		
Farmers	4703	70.7
Production workers	1099	16.5
Commercial/service workers	448	6.7
Administrators/office-related workers	80	1.2
Scientists/Technicians	324	4.9
Family Annual Income (yuan)		
Less than 1000	1139	18.5
1000 to 1999	1929	31.3
2000 to 2999	1189	19.3
3000 to 3999	866	14.0
4000 or more	1049	17.0

Total percentage may not be 100% due to rounding errors, and total numbers
of cases may vary because of missing data

Chinese women as a group were less educated than their male counterparts. Only one percent of the respondents obtained education beyond high school. Yet slightly less than 23 percent of them were illiterate compared to 4.5 percent of their husbands. The average year of education was 4.6 for the female respondents and 7.1 for their husbands.

Residence, rural or urban, is an important aspect for understanding Chinese society and individual behavior, partially because of a huge gap between rural and urban lifestyles and partially because of the limited geographic mobility in China. In this regard, as shown in the table, the majority (78.7 percent) of the respondents in the survey were rural residents. This distribution was somewhat consistent with the results from the Population Censuses. The percentage of rural residents in China was 73.8 in the 1982 Census and 73.7 in the 1990 Census (The State Statistical Bureau, 1990).

China has more than 55 minority nationalities, and they are different from Han majority in terms of demographic and socioeconomic compositions (Poston and Shu, 1987). As anticipated, the overwhelming majority (97.5 percent) of the respondents in the IDFS sample were Han women. This distinction is particularly crucial because minority ethnic groups in China are not subject to the strict family planning policies (Park and Han, 1990).

In terms of occupation, over 70 percent of the respondents were farmers. About 16.5 percent worked in factories as production workers, and 6.7 percent worked in commercial or service sectors. Only slightly over one percent of the respondents were administrators or office-related workers. Slightly less than five percent were scientists or technicians. In addition, nearly one-half of the respondents reported an annual income of less than ¥2,000. Some 17 percent of the families surveyed lived with an income of ¥ 4,000 or more.

Sample distributions regarding marriage and fertility are listed in Table 4.2. More than 98 percent of the women responding to the survey were currently married and 96.4 percent of them were still in their first marriage. Yet the ages at first marriage varied, ranging from 11 to 37 years old. More than 30 percent of the responding women married before reaching their twentieth year

Table 4.2

Sample Descriptions on Marriage and Fertility, IDFS Data

Marriage/Fertility Characteristics	Number	Percentage
Marital Status		
Current married	6541	98.3
Divorced/separated/widowed	113	1.7
Still in First Marriage		
Yes	6416	96.4
No	238	3.6
Age at First Marriage		
17 or younger	645	9.7
18 to 19 years old	1392	20.9
20 to 22 years old	2376	35.7
23 to 24 years old	1252	18.8
25 or older	989	14.9
Time of First Marriage		
1971 or earlier (before WXS)	2346	38.0
1972 to 1979 (WXS period)	1917	31.1
1980 to 1982 (1st one-child period)	957	15.5
1983 to 1987 (2nd one-child period)	952	15.4
Living with Husband's Parents		
Never	1636	24.6
Lived with them before	3046	45.8
Living with them now	1972	29.6
Living with Wife's Parents		
Never	6266	94.2
Lived with them before	211	3.2
Living with them now	177	2.7
Number of Living Children		
None	399	6.0
One	1354	20.3
Two	1779	26.7
Three	1545	23.2
Four	927	13.9
Five or more	650	9.8

Total percentage may not be 100% due to rounding errors.

birthday. The majority of the women married in their earlier 20s (20-24 years old), and less than 15 percent were married at age 25 or older.

The year of marriage is grouped according to the periods of several family planning campaigns in China. As shown in the table, more than one-third of the respondents married before the "Later-Longer-Fewer" campaign of 1971. Slightly more than 30 percent married during the "Later-Longer-Fewer" period. Another one-third respondents married after the implementation of the "One-Child" family planning policy, and a half of them married after 1982 when the "One-Child" policy was modified.

Regarding the living arrangements after marriage, married couples traditionally live with the husband's families. More than three-fourths of the respondents lived with their husbands' families after their marriage, compared to only about six percent who lived with the wives' families. This distribution reflects a pattern of living arrangements after marriage in China (Arnold and Liu, 1986; Wasserstrom, 1987).

As Table 4.2 shows, 94 percent of the respondents reported having children. Approximately one-fifth of the respondents had only one child and slightly more than one-fourth, or 26.7 percent, had two children. About 23 percent indicated that they had three children, and another 13.9 percent reported four living children. Slightly less than 10 percent of the respondents had five or more children. The average number of living children was 2.5.

Sample Description of OASS Data

The Old-Age Security Survey contained 220 rural married couples. As shown in Table 4.3, husbands as a group were older than their wives. Some 47.7 percent of the wives were in their 30s, compared to the same percentage of husbands aged 40 or older. More than 12 percent of the wives were 29 years old or younger, while 8.6 percent of the husbands fell in this category.

Consistent with the IDFS data, there was a big gap in educational attainment between Chinese women and their husbands. Some 15.5 percent of the wives were illiterate, compared to 1.4 percent in the husband sample. About 31.6 percent of the husbands had high school education, while only 6.8 percent of the wives had the same educational level.

Table 4.3

Sample Descriptions on Demographic Characteristics, OASS Data

Demographic Characteristics	Number	Percentage
Wife's Age		
29 years old or younger	27	12.3
30 to 39 years old	105	47.7
40 years old or older	88	40.0
Husband's Age		
29 years old or younger	19	8.6
30 to 39 years old	96	43.6
40 years old or older	105	47.7
Wife's Education		
No schooling	34	15.5
1 to 6 years	171	77.7
7 to 12 years	15	6.8
Husband's Education		
No schooling	3	1.4
1 to 6 years	146	67.0
7 to 12 years	69	31.6

Total percentage may not be 100% due to rounding errors, and total numbers of cases may vary because of missing data.

Marriage and fertility characteristics of the OASS data are presented in Table 4.4. More than a half of the respondents married between the ages of 20

Table 4.4
Sample Descriptions on Marriage and Fertility, OASS Data

Marriage/Fertility Characteristics	Number	Percentage
Age at First Marriage		
19 years old or younger	9	4.1
20 to 22 years old	70	31.8
23 to 24 years old	50	22.7
25 to 27 years old	63	28.6
28 years old or older	28	12.7
Still in First Marriage		
Yes	179	81.4
No	41	18.6
Time of First Marriage		
1971 or earlier (before WXS)	90	41.5
1972 to 1979 (WXS period)	61	28.1
1980 to 1982 (1st one-child period)	34	15.7
1983 to 1987 (2nd one-child period)	32	14.7
Living with Husband's Parents Now		
Yes	36	21.3
No	133	78.7
Living with Wife's Parents Now		
Yes	4	2.2
No	177	97.8
Number of Living Children		
None	5	2.3
One	33	15.0
Two	93	42.3
Three	51	23.2
Four	26	11.8
Five or more	12	5.5

Total percentage may not be 100% due to rounding errors, and total numbers of cases may vary because of missing data.

to 24. Approximately 41 percent of the women had their first marriage when they were 25 or older, and slightly more than four percent married for the first time before their 20 year birthdays. Most women in the survey were still in their first marriage, comprising 81.4 percent of the wife sample.

Of the responding couples, about 41.5 percent married before the "Later-Longer-Fewer" campaign, and approximately 28 percent married during the campaign. More than 30 percent of the respondents married after the implementation of the one-child family planning policy, and less than a half of them married after the policy modification.

Similar to the IDFS data, more married couples lived with husbands' parents than with wives' families. About 21.3 percent of the couples were living with husbands' parents during the time the survey was conducted, while only 2.2 percent of the sample were living with wives' families.

In terms of the number of children, only about 2.3 percent of the couples had no children. Some 15 percent of the couples had only one child, while more than 42 percent had two. Slightly over 23 percent reported that they had three children and another 11.8 percent reported four. About 5.5 percent of the couples who responded to the survey had five or more children. The average number of children was 2.4, which paralleled to the number reported in the IDFS sample.

STUDY SETTING

All data sources are from one province in China - Guangdong. In order to understand the background and the representation of the data, it is necessary to briefly examine the research site with respect to its environmental and socioeconomic conditions, fertility trends, and family planning efforts.

Environmental and Socioeconomic Background

Guangdong is located on the southern coast of China (see Figure 4.1), a semitropical province with the size of 212,550 square kilometers and with a population of 62.83 million in 1990. Guangdong is agriculturally very rich and full of a range of minerals, coal, and metals. Because its location is

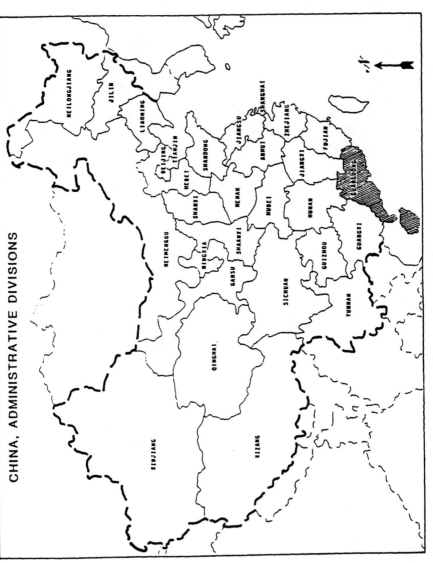

Figure 4.1 Map of People's Republic of China

adjacent to Hong Kong, the province has always been the forefront of China's relations with the outside world (Vogel, 1989).

Guangdong is divided into eight municipal regions, three prefectures, and one autonomous region, a total of 93 counties and 16 cities (see Figure 4.2). The urban population counts about 36.77 percent of the total population, and approximately 99.4 percent of the population belong to the Han majority (Guangdong Statistical Bureau, 1990).

The economic reforms after 1978 have allowed Guangdong to take advantage of new opportunities and to accelerate changes. In 1991 the economy of Guangdong grew faster than nearly any other in the world - 27.2 percent (Gibney, 1992). The standard of living in Guangdong is ranked as one of the highest in China (McGregor, 1991).

Fertility Trends in Guangdong Province

Generally speaking, the fertility trends between Guangdong and China are quite parallel, as illustrated in Figure 4.3. The fluctuations during the 1950s and 1960s are closely related to political and natural disasters that occurred during that period. Following the general fertility trend of China, Guangdong had achieved a substantial drop in fertility by 1970, and then continued to drop until 1977.

In the late 1970s and early 1980s, however, Guangdong showed resistance to the family planning program. The fertility rates of Guangdong had been consistently higher than the national average until the late 1980s. According to the statistics issued by the National Statistic Bureau of China, Guangdong was one of the few provinces with high "out-of-plan" fertility rates in 1988 (The State Statistical Bureau, 1989). As Judith Banister put it, "Guangdong is the best example so far of a popular backlash against China's increasingly restrictive family planning program" (Banister, 1987: 285).

Family Planning Programs in Guangdong Province

The family planning programs of Guangdong had been effective since the 1960s. Yet, it was not until the provincial family planning meeting in 1970 that family planning efforts became more institutionalized and widespread.

56

Li Li

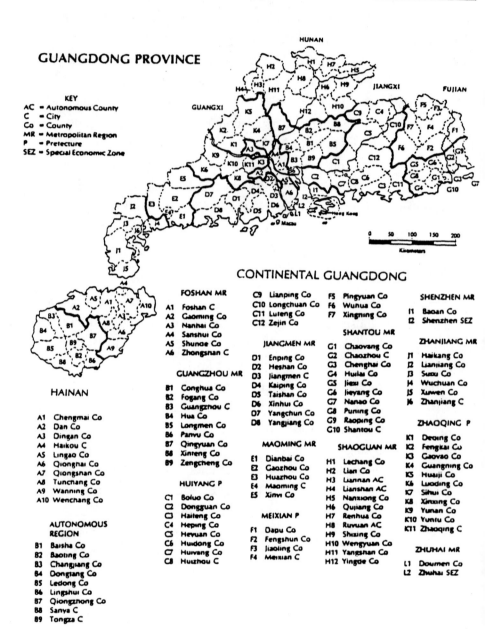

Figure 4.2 Map of Guangdong Province, China

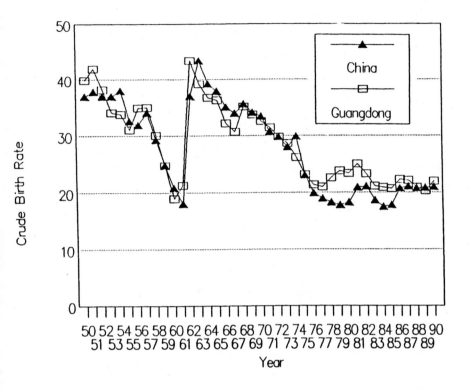

Figure 4.3 Fertility Trends of Guangdong and China

By 1978 there were 2,000 family planning technicians at county-level, about 8,000 trained family planning personnel at commune-level, and about 50,000 at brigade-level. In 1983 family planning expenditure for the province was approximately one billion yuans (Zhu, 1986).

Guangdong's family planning programs follow the general patterns of the national policies. During the "Later-Longer-Fewer" campaign initiated in 1971, married couples in Guangdong were limited to having two children in cities and three in rural areas. At the time when the one-child policy was announced nationwide in 1979, Guangdong also applied the "one couple, one child" regulation. Nevertheless, at the end of 1982 the Guangdong family planning commission modified its one-child policies by being more permissive toward second children among rural couples whose first child was a daughter and families with "real difficulties." In 1984 this lenient policy was adopted at a national level, written in the Central Document 7 (Bongaarts, 1985; Greenhalgh, 1986; Zhu, 1986).

Significance of Guangdong Setting

Guangdong somewhat "deviates" from the rest of the country in terms of its rapid economic development and its poor family planning performance. This phenomenon appears contradictory to the demographic transition theory, which assumes a negative relationship between socioeconomic development and fertility.

In spite of the variations, however, the representation of Guangdong remains significant. First, fertility trends over the past four decades in the province followed the trends of the whole country. Second, "out-of-plan" fertility in Guangdong is better documented than that in other parts of China (Banister, 1987). Third, in terms of policy implications, Guangdong appears important for further implementations of family planning programs. Guangdong has been set up as a model province for the remainder of the country in terms of economic development. The more permissive family planning policies of Guangdong were expanded into other provinces in 1984. For this reason, studying "out-of-plan" fertility in Guangdong will have implications for the whole country in the future.

MEASUREMENT

Deviant Fertility

As a major dependent variable, deviant fertility (DF) was measured in terms of the discrepancies between the actual number of children a couple had (B) and the number allowed by the family planning policies (Bp). As a general rule, if the birth of a particular couple surpassed the number that the family policy permitted, this birth was considered as deviant fertility.

Given that family planning policies in China change over different periods and are applied to rural and urban areas differently, the time frame (t) and the residence (r) must be taken into account in measuring deviant fertility. For instance, the second birth of a rural couple was not regarded as unsanctioned until the early 1980s. In addition, since there are different family planning policies for minority groups and for those who are remarried, deviant fertility here only pertained for those respondents who were Han and still in their first marriage.

Taking these components into account, deviant fertility was measured with the following formula:

$$DF = 1, \text{ IF } B > Bp_{[t,r]}$$
$$DF = 0, \text{ IF } B \; Bp_{[t,r]}$$

Where

DF   Deviant fertility

B   Actual number of births

$Bp_{[t,r]}$ Number of planned births subject to time and residence

Independent Variables in the OASS Data

In addition to deviant fertility, a number of variables were defined and measured in the Old-Age Security Survey data. The detailed measurements are listed in Table 4.5.

Expectations of Benefits from Children (BENEFIT). Measuring the norm constraints on individuals is extremely difficult because of the deficiency of direct indicators. However, as a latent variable, norm constraints can be measured by relevant indicators. By using the OASS data, the traditional fertility norm constraints were measured by the expectations of benefits from children when parents get old. The expectation was defined as perceptions by parents on children's responsibilities for the older generation. It is reasonable to anticipate that a high expectation of benefits from children reflects the traditional fertility ideal.

Specifically, the expectation of benefits from children was measured by a scale (designated as BENEFIT) including nine questions. The respondents, both wives and husbands, were asked to reply whether they required their children to do the following: 1) send money to parents; 2) visit parents

Li Li

Table 4.5

Variable Descriptions, OASS Data

Variables	Descriptions	Mean	Std. Dev.
Expectation of benefits from Children (BENEFIT)	10 point scale ranged from 0 to 9	6.96	1.73
Living standard (LIVING)	11 point scale ranged from 3 to 13	7.67	1.71
Family sizes of origin (SIZE)	11 point scale ranged from 1 to 11	5.59	2.16
Relation with parents (CLOSE)	10 point scale ranged from 2 to 11	6.52	2.73
Previous female births (ALLGIRL)	Dummy variable 1=All female births 0=Otherwise	0.28	0.45
Educational attainment (EDUC)	7 point scale ranged from 1 to 7	2.74	1.01
Number of children (CHILD)	6 point scale ranged from 0 to 5	2.43	1.12
Number of sons (SON)	6 point scale ranged from 0 to 5	1.30	0.96
Number of daughters (GIRL)	6 point scale ranged from 0 to 5	1.14	1.03

frequently; 3) live with parents; 4) uphold parents' "faces"; 5) be successful at work; 6) let parents enjoy luxury; 7) provide parents enough living support; 8) visit when parents are ill; and 9) respect parents. Some other relevant items were deleted in this study because they were closely related to the gender of children, such as "give births of grandsons" and "help with housework." Each item in the scale had the same weight and was added together, resulting in a scale of 10 points ranged from zero to nine. The higher the number, the higher the expectations of benefits from children. The reliability of the scale was tested by Cronbach's alpha. The test for this nine-item scale showed an overall alpha reliability coefficient of .63.

Living Standard (LIVING). Living standard was defined as a combination of both economic and living conditions. The scale included three questions. First, the respondents were asked to evaluate their overall economic situations. The replies were: "Upper," "Middle upper," "Middle," "Lower middle," and "Low." The second question came from observations and evaluations by interviewers on interviewees' living conditions. The same responding categories from "Upper" to "Low" were applied. Finally, a question on the types of houses was included in the scale, and the responses ranged from "One-story house" to "Four-story house." After adding the three questions, the scale ranged from 3 to 13. A higher score suggests a better living condition. The reliability coefficient of this three-item scale is .69.

Family Sizes of Origin (SIZE). Family sizes of origin was defined as the number of children in the family of origin. The variable was summarized from the census type questions. Among those 220 married couples who responded to the survey, the average number of children in their families of origin was 5.6, ranging from one to 11.

Relations with Parents (CLOSE). The relationship between the respondents and their parents was defined as the frequencies with which respondents kept in touch with their parents. The respondents were asked to reply whether they visited their parents "At least once a week," "Once a week," "Once a month," "Occasionally," or "Never." Another similar question was asked on how often their parents visited the respondents, with the same responses categories. A 10-point scale was computed after the two questions were added. The higher the score, the more frequent the interactions with parents. For those who lived with their parents in the same household, the score of 11 was assigned.

Previous Female Births (ALLGIRL). A dummy variable was used to measure whether all previous births were females. Here, previous births refer to those living children prior to the last one by the time of the survey in 1987. Regardless of the number of children, the dummy variable was one if all previous births were females. For example, if a couple had five children and the previous four were all females, ALLGIRL was specified as one. If one of the previous four children was a son, however, a zero was assigned.

Educational Attainment (EDUC). Educational attainment was recorded into seven categories: "Illiterate," "Primary school," "Secondary school," "Junior high school," "Senior high school," and "Technical school." Here both formal and informal education were included.

Age at Marriage (MAGE). Age at first marriage was ascertained by exact age. The average age at the first marriage in the sample of 440 husbands and wives was 25 years old.

Independent Variables in the IDFS Data

Variables used for analyzing the IDFS data are illustrated in Table 4.6 and 4.7. Table 4.6 presents the descriptions of county-level and individual-level variables on socioeconomic and demographic characteristics. The county-level variables on socioeconomic development were derived from the 1982 Census, and the data of monetary input of family planning were collected specifically for this study. As background variables, the county-level indicators were merged with individual respondents in the IDFS data. Table 4.7 describes indicators of marriage, previous reproductive experiences, and family planning.

Differentiated from the OASS data that included both husbands and wives as separate respondents, the IDFS data contained only information about ever-married women. In addition, questions in the IDFS data were much more comprehensive and far-reaching than those in the OASS data.

Per Capita Industrial and Agricultural Output (PRODCTY). Per capita values of industrial and agricultural output were used to assess the levels of productivity, measured in an exact amount of money (¥). As shown in Table 4.6, the values of per capita industrial and agriculture output produced by each county ranged from ¥225 to ¥4,082, reflecting the fact that productivity varied tremendously over different counties.

Levels of Industrialization (INDUSTRY). An industrialization scale was created by combining the percentages of industrial and non-agricultural employment population. The higher the score, the higher the level of industrialization. Again, Cronbach's alpha was used to test its reliability, resulting in a high alpha value of .97.

Levels of Education (EDUCLVL). Two indicators were combined and used to measure educational levels for various counties. The first item was the percentage of illiterate/semi-illiterate for persons aged 12 or older, while the second was the number of persons with junior/middle school education per 10,000 people. The two variables were converted into the same direction and measurement unit, and, then, combined into a single scale. The alpha reliability of this scale was .84.

Macro Socioeconomic Conditions (MACROSEC). The macro socioeconomic condition was a summarized index that included three individual scales: per capita gross values of industrial and agricultural output (PRODCTY), levels of industrialization (INDUSTRY), and levels of education (EDUCLVL). Specifically, the index was computed as follows:

MACROSEC = Zscore(PRODCTY) + Zscore(INDUSTRY) + Zscore(EDUCLVL)

A factor analysis was performed on these three variables. The procedure extracted only one factor for the scale, and 47.5 percent of the variations in the scale can be explained by this factor. The Cronbach's alpha coefficient for this index was placed at .85.

Monetary Input in Family Planning (MONEY). Monetary input in family planning, defined as the amount of money per person that the government spent in family planning uses in 1987, was used to measure family planning efforts made by various counties. The scale ranged from ¥0.46 to ¥2.78 per person, with a mean value of ¥1.07 per person per year spending on family planning.

Educational Attainment (EDUC/HEDUC). Educational levels for both the respondents and their husbands were measured in exact years completed. As presented in Table 4.6, the scale ranged from zero to 17 years for the

Table 4.6

Descriptions of County-Level and Individual-level Variables on
Socioeconomic Characteristics, IDFS Data

Variables	Descriptions	Mean	Std. Dev
Per capita gross values of output (Y)	A scale ranged from		
(PRODCTY)	225 to 4082	878.8	964.9
Levels of industrialization	A scale ranged		
(INDUSTRY)	from 5.65 to 64.70	22.99	18.12
Educational levels	A scale ranged		
(EDUCLVL)	from 35.81 to 58.04	48.53	5.52
Macro socioeconomic conditions	A scale ranged		
(MACROSEC)	from -3.62 to 6.84	0.00	2.64
Monetary input on family planning (Y)	A scale ranged		
(MONEY)	from 0.46 to 2.78	1.07	0.46
Educational attainments (years)	A scale ranged		
(EDUC)	from 0 to 17	4.61	3.73
Husbands' educational attainments	A scale ranged		
(HEDUC)	from 0 to 18	7.08	3.47
Occupational prestige	A scale ranged		
(OCCUP)	from 22 to 78	26.99	10.53
Husbands' occupational prestige	A scale ranged		
(HOCCUP)	from 22 to 78	31.29	13.30
Annual family income (Y)	A scale ranged		
(INCOME)	from 60 to 84000	2611	2523
Individual socioeconomic status	A scale ranged		
(SES)	from -5.40 to 32.51	0.09	3.41
Types of employment	A dummy variable		
(EMPLOYER)	1=State owned;		
	0=Others	0.22	0.42
Parents' educational attainments	9 point scale		
(PAMAEDUC)	ranged from 1 to 5	1.51	0.53
Residence	A dummy variable		
(RURAL)	1=Rural; 0=Urban	0.78	0.41

respondents and zero to 18 for their husbands. In addition, the average year of education was 4.6 for the respondents and about seven for their husbands.

Occupational Prestige (OCCUP/HOCCUP). Occupational prestige was measured according to Treiman's Standard International Occupational Prestige Scale (Treiman, 1977). In fact, occupational prestige in China had not been investigated in recent years until an article published by Lin and Xie (1988). Comparing the rank ordering of prestige in urban China and other countries, Lin and Xie (1988) reported that the correlation coefficient between the Chinese score and the Treiman scale was .90. In this study, the Treiman scale was used to measure both the respondents' and their husbands' occupational prestige. As indicated in Table 4.6, the average score for the respondents was lower than that of their husbands.

Annual Family Income (INCOME). Annual family income was used to measure a family's economic well-being. As shown in Table 4.6, there exists a vast gap between the highest and the lowest income in the sample, ranging from ¥60 to ¥84,000.

Individual Socioeconomic Status (SES). There are various indicators of socioeconomic status in the literature, including multiple-item approaches and single-item indicators. Multiple-item measurements are beneficial because they take into account the different dimensions of socioeconomic conditions (Nam and Powers, 1983). Individual socioeconomic status in this study was a concise measure, including a respondent's education, her husband's education, a respondent's occupational prestige, her husbands' occupational prestige, and annual family income. The indicators were standardized first and added together with the same weight by the following formula:

$$SES = Zscore(EDUC) + Zscore(HEDUC) + Zscore(OCCUP) + Zscore(HOCCUP) + Zscore(INCOME)$$

The reliability level of this five-item scale was placed at the alpha value of .71.

Type of Employment (EMPLOYER). In addition to income, type of employment is also an indicator of family economic well-being and benefits. Basically, there are three types of employment in China: state-owned, collective, and individual. Additionally, types of employment are also related to the implementation of family planning in China. Those who work in the stated-own sector such as government officers, school teachers, workers in state-owned factories, for example, bear more severe punishments for violations of family planning policies than those in the collective or individual sectors. In this study, the type of employment was measured as a dummy variable. Those respondents or their husbands who work in the state-owned sector were counted as one, and those who identified with the collective or individual employments were measured as zero.

Parents' Education (PAMAEDUC). Parents' educational levels were used as a proxy for family backgrounds. In the original questionnaires, fathers' and mothers' educational levels were requested separately. The choice of answers ranged from 1=No schooling to 5=University/higher. The two questions were added together with the same weight and then divided by two, resulting in a scale measuring educational levels of respondents' parents.

Residence (RURAL). Residence was defined as the type of residing place when the survey was conducted. Administratively, two types of urban place exist in China: city (shi) and town (zhen). A large municipality, however, also administers a number of counties (xian). As the boundary between urban and rural is rather confusing, the problem has been named as a "demographic mystery." Nevertheless, in most cases "urban residents" only refer to those non-agricultural people who register an urban residence as their domicile (Chan and Xu, 1985). The variable of residence in this study was dichotomous. A value of one was assigned for rural residents and zero for urban non-agricultural people living in either cities or towns.

Age at First Marriage (MAGE). Age at first marriage was recorded by the exact age when a respondent was married. Since only those still in the first marriage were included in this study, the variable represented the marriage age in general. As shown in Table 4.7, marriage ages ranged from 11 to 37 years old.

Living with Parents After Marriage (LIVEWITH). Living with parents after marriage was regarded not only as an indicator of living arrangements by married couples but also, more importantly, as a potential factor related to fertility outcomes in terms of the influence of older generations. In this study, living with parents after marriage was defined as either those couples who lived with husbands' parents at least a year after marriage or those who were still living together. The criterion was chosen based on the assumption that some couples might live with parents temporarily for several months after marriage. The dummy variable was given zero to the couples never living with husbands' parents or living with them for less than a year.

Children Death (DEADCHD). Unfortunate reproductive experiences may encourage couples to have a large number of children in order to secure the desired number of their offspring. In this study, child death was defined as the number of dead children that a respondent ever had prior to the survey. The number of dead children in the sample ranged from zero to five.

Terminated Pregnancy Not Due to Family Planning (FAILPREG). Terminated pregnancies that were not due to family planning were also an indicator measuring unfortunate reproductive experiences. The variable was defined as the number of abortions or ended pregnancies resulting from illnesses, miscarriages, stillbirths, or reasons other than family planning. This variable ranged from zero to five.

Previous Female Births (ALLGIRL). Previous female births were measured in terms of all previous births who were female. Here, previous births referred to those living children prior to the last one up to the current survey in 1987. If all the previous children were female, the dummy variable of previous female births was one and zero otherwise.

Several indicators were used to measure family planning pressures, including variables such as knowledge of contraception, abortions because of family planning policies, whether local family planning personnel have contacted the couple individually regarding how many children they should have, and discussions between couples about the number of children. These variables were used individually as proxies for measuring the strength of family planning influences.

Knowledge of Birth Control (KNOW). Knowledge of birth control was defined as the extent to which a respondent was aware of family planning techniques. The respondents were asked if they ever knew such techniques as

Table 4.7
Descriptions of Marriage, Reproductive Experiences, and
Other Deviant Fertility Related Variables, IDFS Data

Variables	Descriptions	Mean	Std. Dev
Age at first marriage (years) (MAGE)	A scale ranged from 11 to 37	21.36	3.17
Living with parents after marriage (LIVEWITH)	A dummy variable 1=Yes; 0=No	0.70	0.46
Number of Children died (DEADCHD)	A scale ranged from 0 to 5	0.15	0.45
Terminated pregnancies not due to family planning (FAILPREG)	A scale ranged from 0 to 5	0.27	0.60
Previous female births (ALLGIRL)	A dummy variable 1=Yes; 0=No	0.18	0.39
Knowledge on birth control (KNOW)	A scale ranged from 0 to 18	8.29	3.61
Number of abortions because of family planning (ABORT)	A scale ranged from 0 to 6	0.25	0.60
Contacted by family planning personnel (CONTACT)	A dummy variable 1=Yes; 0=No	0.43	0.49
Discussing with husbands (DISCUSS)	A dummy variable 1=Yes; 0=No	0.26	0.44
Arranged marriage by parents or others (ARRANGE)	A dummy variable 1=Yes; 0=No	0.10	0.30
Ideal of large family sizes (LARGE)	A scale ranged from 0 to 9	1.29	1.07
Ideal of early marriage (EARLY)	A scale ranged from 0 to 7	0.80	1.13
Son preference for next child (SONPREF)	A dummy variable 1=Yes; 0=No	0.63	0.49

the pill, IUD, female scientific[7], condom, withdrawal, rhythm, injection, female sterilization, or male sterilization as birth control measures. The original responses categories were converted to 0=Don't know, 1=Know after being prompted by interviewers, and 2=Know without being prompted. A scale of knowledge of birth control was computed by combining all answers on the nine questions. Consequently, the knowledge scale (KNOW) varied from 0 to 18, with a mean of 8.3. The Cronbach's alpha test was conducted to assess the reliability of the scale, resulting in a fairly high coefficient of .78.

Abortion Because of Family Planning (ABORT). Abortion because of family planning was defined as the number of abortions a respondent ever had because of family planning. The variable was measured by two items that read: "Do you ever have abortion because of family planning?" "If yes, how many times?" A variable was measured with a range from zero to six.   *Contacts by Family Planning Personnel* (CONTACT). The pressures from family planning programs on individual couples were, in part, measured by personal contacts of family planning representatives. The variable was defined by using the question: "Did local family planning representatives tell you how many children you should have when you got married?" Again, a dummy variable was used with 1=Yes and 0=No.

Discussions with Husbands on Number of Children (DISCUSS). A female respondent's participation in fertility discussions was defined as whether or not she discussed with her husband about how many children they wanted. It was surprising to note that the majority of Chinese women in the sample did not participate in the discussion. Again, a dummy variable was recorded as one for those wives who participated in fertility discussions with their husbands and zero otherwise.

Like the case of family planning pressures, constraints from traditional fertility norms were also measured by several indicators. Included were arranged marriage, the ideal of large family sizes, the ideal of early marriage, and son preference for the next child, which were proxies to measure how strongly the traditional family and fertility norms constrain the respondents.

---

[7] Female scientific measures include spermicide suppository, films, sponges, cream, foam, and diaphragms.

Arranged Marriage by Parents or Others (ARRANGE). Whether a respondent's marriage was arranged was utilized as an indicator of the restrictions from traditional family norms. Respondents were asked if their marriages were arranged by their parents or others. Here, arranged marriage was defined as the marriage that was arranged only by parents and others, coded as one in the dummy variable.

Ideal of Large Family Sizes (LARGE). The measure of the ideal of large family sizes was derived from a question that read "If the present government policy had not existed, how many children would you personally like to have?" The number of children desired was then compared to the baseline number of two. The number of two was selected because this was the tolerable number imposed by the family planning policies. The discrepancy between the two numbers was used as an approximate indicator for the traditional ideal of large family sizes. With a range from zero to nine, the larger the number, the stronger the ideal of large family sizes.

Ideal of Early Marriage (EARLY). The traditional ideal of early marriage was also an approximate measure of traditional normative constraints. With the question "What do you think of the best age for women to get married?" the given ideal age was compared to the age of 22. If the desired age was older than 22, the ideal of early marriage was zero. If, for example, the given age was 17, the score was five.

Son Preference for Next Child (SONPREF). Son preference for the next child was measured by a single question answered only by those respondents who wanted to have another child at the time the survey was conducted. The question was posed, "If you want to have another child in the future, do you prefer to have a boy or a girl?" A dummy variable was used, with the value of one for boy and zero for girl. The inclusion of this variable resulted in a significant decrease in the sample size in analysis.

STATISTICAL ANALYSES

Descriptive statistics were conducted to briefly describe a population or sample. By using graphs and cross-tabulation, the trends and distributions of the patterns examined were illustrated and explicated.

In order to examine the preliminary zero-order relationships of all the independent and dependent variables, simple bivariate analyses such as Pearson's Correlation and Analysis of Variance (ANOVA) were used. These statistics were used to test the strength and the directions of relationships.

To account for the simultaneous effects of the selected independent variables on the dependent variable, multiple regression analyses were employed. The multiple regression analyses were carried out in terms of various equations, or models. Standardized regression coefficients (ß), tests of significance, and coefficients of determination (R^2) were reported for each independent variable or model. The impact of each independent factor on the dependent variable was assessed by controlling other variables.

Based on the bivariate and multivariate analyses, a path model was established. Path analysis is not a method for uncovering causes, but it offers patterns of interpretation of relationships through testing theoretical assumptions (Duncan, 1966; Wolfle, 1980; 1989). Specifically, path analysis was used in this study to decompose associations into components, to illustrate the direct and indirect effects of selected independent variables on deviant fertility, and to examine possible mediating factors in predicting deviant fertility.

CHAPTER V

RESULTS OF THE STUDY

This chapter has three sections. The first section provides a demographic description of deviant fertility in China, including information from the fertility survey (IDFS), the old-age security survey (OASS), and the records of the family planning commission (RCFPC). The second section presents results of the OASS data, focusing on the effects of family backgrounds, expectations of benefits from children, traditional family ideals as well as demographic characteristics on deviant fertility. The third section deals with results from the fertility survey data. Through bivariate and multivariate analyses, including path analyses, relationships among identified variables are examined and the hypotheses stated earlier are tested.

DESCRIPTIVE ANALYSIS

Results from RCFPC Data

The records of Panyu County Family Planning Commission reveal the official version of fertility trends and incidences of "out-of-plan" fertility. The materials are summarized and illustrated by several graphics.

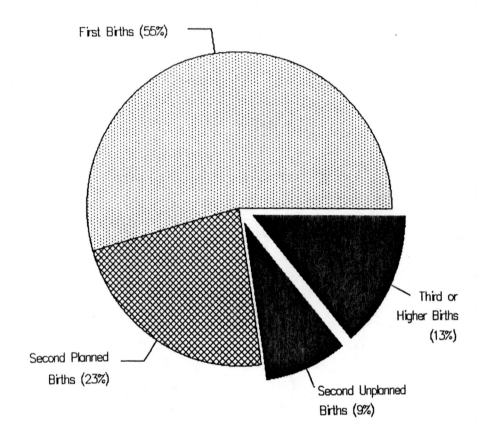

Figure 5.1 Fertility Distribution by Birth Order, RCFPC Data

Figure 5.1 presents the average birth order distributions over the period
from 1988 to 1990. Among the total births in this three years, over one-half (55
percent) were first births, slightly less than one-third (32 percent) were second
order births, and about 13 percent third or higher order births. The distribution
was close to the national average from the 1990 census in which the first birth
accounted for 49.5 percent of total births, 31.2 percent for the second order,
and 19.3 the third or higher order births in 1989 (Population Census Office,
1991).

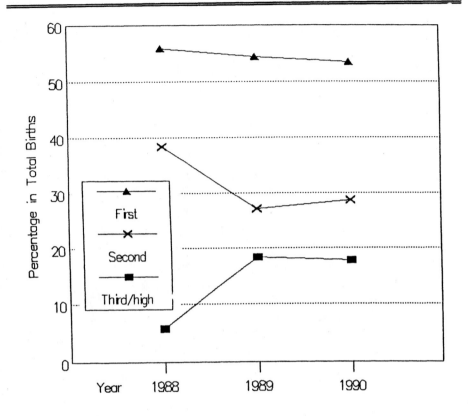

Figure 5.2 Fertility Trends from 1988 to 1990, RCFPC Data

Family planning records provided more details on second order births. According to the population policies, the second order births may be planned or unplanned. As illustrated in Figure 5.1, second planned births made up 23 percent of the total births while second unplanned ones accounted for nine percent. Adding the "out-of-plan" second births to the births of third or higher order, the total "deviant" fertility, on average, comprised approximately 22 percent of the total births.

In addition to the average pattern over a three-year period, fertility by birth order in each year is further depicted. Shown in Figure 5.2, the proportion of first child births remained relatively stable from 1988 to 1990. Substantial changes were found in the second and the third or higher order births from 1988 to 1989. The second births dropped from 38.3 percent in 1988 to 27.2 percent

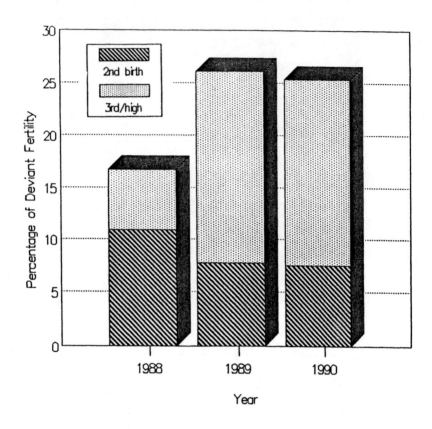

Figure 5.3   Deviant Fertility by Birth Order, RCFPC Data

in 1989, while the third or high order births raised from 5.8 percent in 1988 to 18.4 percent in 1989.

Related to the general fertility trends by birth order, the percentage of total "out-of-plan" births jumped in 1989. Figure 5.3 presents the proportion of the second births and that of the third or higher order births in making up the total deviant fertility. In 1988 the second births counted for about two-thirds of the total deviant fertility. With the increase of higher order births in 1989, the "out-of-plan" second order births only made up less than one-third of the total deviant fertility. The majority of "out-of-plan" fertility came from the third and higher order births. The proportion remained about the same for 1990.

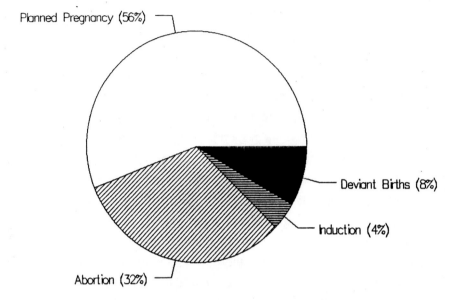

Figure 5.4 Types of Pregnancy and Outcomes, RCFPC Data

"Out-of-plan" fertility results from "out-of-plan" pregnancy. Figure 5.4 shows the percentage distribution in types of pregnancy and outcomes in the three-year period. Pregnancies according to the family planning policies only comprised slightly more than one-half of the total pregnancy. Approximately two-third of the "out-of-plan" pregnancies resulted in abortions, and more than nine percent were terminated by inductions[8]. As a result, about 18 percent of "out-of-plan" pregnancies, or eight percent of the total pregnancy, led to deviant fertility.

Descriptive Results from IDFS Data

In order to understand fertility behavior of those couples with "out-of-plan" births, it is necessary to examine their demographic attributes, compared to their "planned" counterparts. The respondents in the comparison were limited to those Han majority women who married after 1971 and were still in their first marriage at the time the survey was conducted. Of the 3,673 respondents, about

---

[8] In China, inductions refer to abortions after three month pregnancy.

one-third had deviant fertility while another two-thirds did not. This number was slightly higher than the official count described earlier.

When rural and urban residents were compared descriptively, it is evident that those who lived in rural areas were more likely to have deviant fertility than urban ones. Some 35.3 percent of rural respondents, compared to 21.2 percent of urban respondents, were in this category. When age was considered, it appeared that 44.4 percent of the respondents aged 30 to 39 were associated with deviant fertility. Because the family planning regulations had not been strict until the 1970's, it is not surprising that the majority of women with deviant fertility were in their 30s.

The fertility deviants, as a group, were relatively less educated. Nearly half of the illiterate respondents, more than one-third of those with primary school education, and less than 22 percent of those with high school education were involved with deviant fertility. It was true for both the responding women and their husbands that, when their educational attainment increased, the percentage of deviant fertility declined.

The data in Table 5.1 also show how family income is related to deviant fertility. Deviant fertility was more likely to occur in low income families than in high income ones. For example, almost 40 percent of the families with less than 1,000 yuan annual incomes had deviant fertility, while only 22.2 percent of the families with 4,000 or more annual income fell in this category. The finding suggests a negative relationship between economic conditions and deviant fertility.

Since the definition of deviant fertility varies in different time periods, Table 5.2 presents results from cross-tabulation of fertility by time of the marriage. Among 1,185 fertility deviants in the sample, 994 married during the "Later-Longer-Fewer" campaign period, comprising 54.2 percent of respondents who married during that time. Only a minority of the respondents who married after 1980 had deviant fertility. This is perhaps due to the relatively short period of time before the survey was conducted

Table 5.1

Percentage Distributions of Deviant and Non-deviant Fertility by
Demographic Characteristics, IDFS Data

Demographic Characteristics	Deviant	Non-deviant
Total*	1185(100.0)/(32.3)	2488(100.0)/(67.7)
Residence		
Rural	1019 (86.0)/(35.3)	1870 (75.2)/(64.7)
Urban	166 (14.0)/(21.2)	618 (24.8)/(78.8)
Age		
17 to 29 years old	337 (28.4)/(19.4)	1403 (56.4)/(80.6)
30 to 39 years old	837 (70.6)/(44.4)	1047 (42.1)/(55.6)
40 to 49 years old	11 (0.9)/(22.4)	38 (1.5)/(77.6)
Education		
No schooling	287 (24.2)/(47.5)	317 (12.7)/(52.5)
1 to 6 years	611 (51.6)/(35.5)	1112 (44.7)/(64.5)
7 to 12 years	287 (24.2)/(21.9)	1021 (41.0)/(78.1)
13 or more years	0 (0.0)/ (0.0)	38 (1.5)/(100.0)
Husband's Education		
No schooling	45 (3.9)/(50.0)	45 (1.8)/(50.0)
1 to 6 years	487 (41.9)/(37.5)	810 (33.0)/(62.5)
7 to 12 years	624 (53.7)/(29.1)	1522 (62.0)/(70.9)
13 or more years	7 (0.6)/ (8.4)	76 (3.1)/(91.6)
Family Annual Income (Yuan)		
Under 1000	288 (24.3)/(39.8)	435 (17.5)/(60.2)
1000 to 1999	428 (36.1)/(36.8)	735 (29.5)/(63.2)
2000 to 2999	216 (18.2)/(31.1)	479 (19.3)/(68.9)
3000 to 3999	123 (10.4)/(24.3)	384 (15.4)/(75.7)
4000 or more	130 (11.0)/(22.2)	455 (18.3)/(77.8)

* The total number included only Han majority people who married after 1971 and
were still in their first marriages in 1987; total number of cases may vary because of
missing data.

Table 5.2

Percentage Distributions of Deviant and Non-deviant Fertility by Time of Marriage,
Age at Marriage, and Number of Children, IDFS Data

	Deviant	Non-deviant
Time of the Marriage		
1972 to 1979 (WXS period)	994 (83.9)/(45.2)	839 (33.7)/(45.8)
1980 to 1982 (1st one-child period)	176 (14.9)/(19.3)	737 (29.6)/(80.7)
1983 to 1987 (2nd one-child period)	15 (1.3)/ (1.6)	912 (36.7)/(98.4)
Age at First Marriage		
17 or younger	64 (5.4)/(37.4)	107 (4.3)/(62.6)
18 to 19 years old	195 (16.5)/(37.1)	331 (13.3)/(62.9)
20 to 22 years old	494 (41.7)/(37.5)	822 (33.0)/(62.5)
23 to 24 years old	269 (22.7)/(30.6)	609 (24.5)/(69.4)
25 or older	163 (13.8)/(20.8)	619 (24.9)/(79.2)
Number of Living Children		
None or one	0 (0.0)/ (0.0)	1310 (52.6)/(100.)
Two	292 (24.6)/(22.6)	1002 (40.3)/(77.4)
Three	589 (49.7)/(77.0)	176 (7.1)/(23.0)
Four or more	304 (25.7)/(100.)	0 (0.0)/ (0.0)
Total*	1185 (100.0)	2488 (100.0)

* The total number included only Han majority people who married after 1971
and were still in their first marriages in 1987.

For the age at marriage, it was found that, of those who married at ages 22 or younger, some 37 percent were identified as fertility deviants. The percentage dropped to 30.6 percent for those who married at ages of 23 to 24, and to 20.8 percent for those who married when they were 25 years old or even older.

Since the number of children is closely related, but not identical, to deviant fertility, it is informative to describe deviant fertility by the number of children. As indicated in Table 5.2, of those who had two children, some 22.6 percent had deviant fertility.

Descriptive Results from OASS Data

Of 220 couples in the OASS data, 130 (58.5 percent) who married after 1971 were included in the descriptive analysis. As shown in Table 5.3, some 20.7 percent of the couples had deviant fertility. Compared to the results from the IDFS data, the percentage of fertility deviancy in the OASS data was relatively low. It was consistent to the IDFS data, however, that the vast majority of fertility deviants were more than thirty years of age. The same trend was found for both the husbands and the wives in terms of age structure and deviant fertility.

Table 5.4 presents data on marriage information by deviant fertility. Approximately 31 percent of the couples who married during the "Later-Longer-Fewer" campaign period were identified with deviant fertility, making up a majority of the total fertility deviants. Again, the relatively long period of time after marriage up to the time the survey was conducted might have contributed to this fact. Moreover, parallel to the IDFS data, deviant fertility was evenly distributed across different age groups of the first marriage. The smallest percentage (14.8 percent) was found among those respondents who married at ages of 22 or younger.

Regarding the number of children, the majority of the couples with two children (86.6 percent) were not identified as fertility deviants. However, over two-thirds of those who have three or more children were associated with deviant fertility, which was consistent with the results of the IDFS data.

Li Li

Table 5.3

Percentage Distribution of Deviant and Non-deviant Fertility by
Demographic Characteristics, OASS Data

Demographic Characteristics	Deviant	Non-deviant
Total*	24(100.0)/(20.7)	92(100.0)/(79.3)
Wife's Age		
29 years old or younger	1 (4.2)/ (4.2)	23 (24.7)/(95.8)
30 to 39 years old	21 (87.5)/(26.9)	57 (61.3)/(73.1)
40 years old or older	2 (8.3)/(13.3)	13 (14.0)/(86.7)
Husband's Age		
29 years old or younger	1 (4.2)/ (5.9)	16 (17.4)/(94.1)
30 to 39 years old	18 (75.0)/(23.7)	58 (63.0)/(76.3)
40 years old or older	5 (20.8)/(21.7)	18 (19.6)/(78.3)
Wife's Education		
No schooling	1 (4.2)/ (9.1)	10 (10.8)/(90.9)
1 to 6 years	20 (83.3)/(21.7)	72 (77.4)/(78.3)
7 to 12 years	3 (12.5)/(21.4)	11 (11.8)/(78.6)
Husband's Education		
No schooling	0 (0.0)/ (0.0)	1 (1.1)/(100.0)
1 to 6 years	17 (70.8)/(24.6)	52 (56.5)/(75.4)
7 to 12 years	7 (29.2)/(15.2)	39 (42.4)/(84.8)
Economic Condition		
Upper or upper middle	1 (4.3)/ (7.7)	12 (14.0)/(92.3)
Middle	13 (56.5)/(35.1)	24 (27.9)/(64.9)
Lower middle	7 (30.4)/(16.7)	35 (40.7)/(83.3)
Low	2 (8.7)/(11.8)	15 (17.4)/(88.2)

* The total number included those couples married after 1971 and were
still in their first marriages in 1987; total number of cases may vary
because of missing data.

Table 5.4

Percentage Distributions of Deviant and Non-deviant Fertility by Time of Marriage, Age at Marriage, and Number of Children, OASS Data

	Deviant	Non-deviant
Time of the Marriage		
1972 to 1979 (WXS period)	19 (79.2)/(31.1)	43 (46.3)/(68.9)
1980 to 1982 (1st one-child period)	4 (16.7)/(17.4)	19 (21.5)/(82.6)
1983 to 1987 (2nd one-child period)	1 (4.2)/ (3.1)	30 (32.3)/(96.9)
Age at the First Marriage		
22 years old or younger	4 (16.7)/(14.8)	23 (25.0)/(85.2)
23 to 24 years old	6 (25.0)/(22.2)	21 (22.8)/(77.8)
25 to 27 years old	9 (37.5)/(23.7)	29 (31.5)/(76.3)
28 years or older	5 (20.8)/(20.8)	19 (20.7)/(79.2)
Number of Living Children		
None to one	0 (0.0)/ (0.0)	29 (31.2)/(100.)
Two	9 (37.5)/(13.4)	58 (62.4)/(86.6)
Three or more	15 (62.5)/(71.4)	6 (6.5)/(28.6)
Total*	24(100.0)/(20.7)	92(100.0)/(79.3)

* The total number included those couples married after 1971 and were still in their first marriages in 1987.

RESULTS OF ANALYZING OASS DATA

Bivariate Findings

The OASS data were further examined using bivariate analyses such as Pearson's Correlation and Analysis of Variance (ANOVA). This was to identify zero-order interrelationships and associations between the relevant variables.

Table 5.5

Comparison of Group Means between Wives and Husbands, OASS Data

Variables	Group Means		Grand Mean	Significance
	Wives	Husbands		
BENEFIT	7.273	6.635	6.954	.000
SIZE	5.532	5.645	5.589	.583
CLOSE	5.609	7.500	6.519	.000
EDUC	2 304	3.188	2.744	.000
MAGE	24.046	25.470	24.758	.000

Total N = 440 individual respondents.

Differences between husbands and wives in fertility-related indicators[9] were inspected first. As presented in Table 5.5, there were significant gender differences in terms of the expectations of benefits from children. After the grand mean was compared with the group means, it was found that wives, as a group, had a significantly higher expectations of benefits from children than their husbands.

Also shown in the table, wives were not significantly different from their husbands in the family sizes of origin. On average, both husbands and wives came from families with five to six children. However, husbands were more likely to have close relationships with their parents than their wives. Given the tradition that women were married out in China, it was not surprising to see this significant difference.

Additionally, as anticipated, the differences between husbands and wives in educational attainment and in the age of first marriage were significant. The

---

[9] Since variables on living standard and previous female birth were shared by the husband and the wife in a family, they were excluded in the comparison.

female respondents had an average level of primary school education, while the mean educational level of their male counterparts was about middle school. The average age of the first marriage was 24 for wives and 25.5 for husbands in the sample.

Table 5.6 summarizes the relationships among fertility-related variables. In general, these variables were not closely correlated with each other, However, several points can be made. First, educational attainment was significantly associated with the expectations of benefits from children (r=-.119). Specifically, those who had higher educational attainment were less likely to have high expectations of benefits from children than those with lower educational levels. Second, the relationship between the expectations of benefits from children and the family sizes of origin was positive and significant (r=.117). The respondents from large families were more likely than those from small families to have a high expectation of benefits from children. Finally, it was discovered that one's relations with parents were significantly associated with his or her educational attainment (r=.170). Relations with parents, however, showed little or no correlation with the expectations of benefits from children.

Table 5.7 presents data on relationships among fertility indicators. Differentiated from the tables shown earlier, the unit of analysis here was households rather than individuals. It is not surprising to see the close association between deviant fertility and the number of children. However, when the total number of children was broken into the numbers of sons and daughters, some fascinating results emerged. Deviant fertility was significantly associated with the number of girls (r=.382), but not with the number of sons (r=.094). In other words, those families with more female children were more likely to be related to deviant fertility than those households with few or no female children.

In a similar manner, deviant fertility was significantly related to families in which all the previous children prior to the last one by 1987 were females. Families with all female previous births were much more likely to be involved with deviant fertility than those otherwise. The association was strong and significant (r=.381). This result indicates a connection between son

Table 5.6

Zero-order Correlation Coefficients Among Expectation for Children, Relation with Parents, Family Sizes of Origin and Demographic Variables, OASS Data

Variables	BENEFIT	EDUC	MAGE	SIZE	CLOSE
BENEFIT	1.000				
EDUC	-.119*	1.000			
MAGE	-.028	.061	1.000		
SIZE	.117*	.005	-.040	1.000	
CLOSE	-.068	.170**	-.104	-.002	1.000

* P < .05;
** P < .01;
*** P < .001.
Total N = 440 individual respondents

Table 5.7

Zero-order Correlation Coefficients Among Fertility Indicators, OASS Data

Variables	DEVIANT	CHILD	SON	GIRL	ALLGIRL
DEVIANT	1.000				
CHILD	.529***	1.000			
SON	.094	.523***	1.000		
GIRL	.382***	.590***	-.331***	1.000	
ALLGIRL	.381***	.117	-.355***	.456***	1.000

* P < .05;
** P < .01;
*** P < .001.
Total N = 220 households.

preference and deviant fertility, which, of course, needs to be further explored. Table 5.8 reveals correlations between fertility indicators and fertility-related variables. It was noted that both educational attainment and the age at first marriage exhibited strongly negative relations with the number of children (r=-.218 and r=-.241, respectively). As suggested by previous studies, the higher the educational level, the less likely a large numbers of children. Also, those who married at early ages were more likely to have more children than those who had their first marriages at later ages.

Table 5.8

Zero-order Correlation Coefficients Among Fertility Indicators and
Fertility-related Variables, OASS Data

Variables	CHILD	SON	GIRL	DEVIANT
BENEFIT	.011	.099*	-.074	-.081
EDUC	-.218***	-.146**	-.111*	-.086
LIVING	.059	.067	.018	-.011
MAGE	-.241***	-.174***	-.108*	.023
SIZE	-.072	-.040	-.054	-.082
CLOSE	-.069	.026	-.077	-.009

* P < .05;

** P < .01;

*** P < .001.

Total N = 440 individual respondents.

Surprisingly, however, no significant association between deviant fertility and selected fertility-related variables was found. It became more interesting to compare how the fertility-related variables were related to the number of children and how they were related to deviant fertility. For example, the age of first marriage was significantly associated with the number of children (r=-.241), but not related to deviant fertility (r=.023). This may suggest that the correlation patterns of deviant fertility differ from those of the number of children, although the two variables are highly correlated.

Another important finding in Table 5.8 consists in the relationship between the expectations of benefits from children and the number of sons as well as the number of daughters. The direction of the expectations of benefits from children relating to the number of sons was in contrast to that of daughters. Specifically, the number of sons was positively and significantly related to parents' expectations of benefits from children (r=.099). However, the expectations were negatively but not significantly associated with the number of female children (r=-.074). In other words, the more male children, the higher the expectations of benefits from children; the more the female children, the lower the parent's expectations of benefits from children.

In order to further examine and depict this issue, two simple regression equations were established to predict the expectations of benefits from children by the number of sons and the number of daughters, respectively. The estimates of regression analyses are illustrated in the following equations:

$$Y^{\text{Expectation}} = 6.722 + .179^{\text{Number of sons}}$$

$$Y^{\text{Expectation}} = 7.097 - .125^{\text{Number of daughters}}$$

The estimated regression lines are illustrated in Figure 5.5. It became clear that the expectations of benefits from children were related to the gender rather than the number of children.

Multivariate Findings

Multivariate analyses in this study used different sets of multiple regression estimations. Since the dependent variable, deviant fertility, was not only dichotomous but also skewed, logistic regression techniques appeared

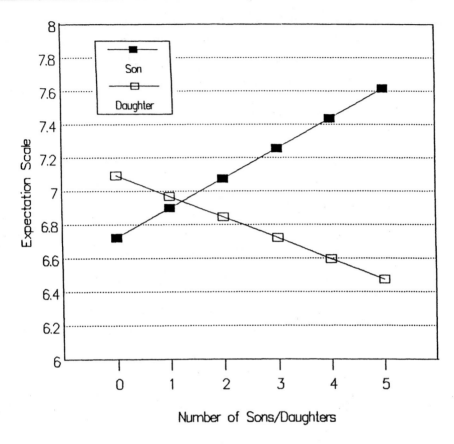

Figure 5.5   Expectation of Benefits From Children, Controlling
Gender of Children, OASS Data

appropriate.[10] In multiple regressions, effects of a predictive factor on deviant fertility could be evaluated independently by controlling other variables.

Table 5.9 presents the results of three regression equations, described as models, for all respondents, wives and husbands, respectively. Because of the purpose of comparison, only variables responded to separately by husbands and wives were included, such as expectation, education, age at first marriage,

---

[10] As suggested by Knoke (1975), logistic regression models are superior to ordinary least square (OLS) on a dichotomous dependent variable in meeting the assumptions of the statistical models. This is particularly true for dependent dummy variables which are extremely skewed (Knoke, 1975).

family sizes of origin, and relations with parents. In Model 1, which included all the respondents, none of the selected variables showed a significant impact on deviant fertility when other variables were controlled. In fact, given the insignificant correlations found in the previous table, the model itself was rather meaningless until compared, as a baseline, to Model 2 and 3.

Table 5.9
Standardized Logistic Regression Coefficients (Beta) of Deviant Fertility
by Fertility-related Variables, OASS Data

Variables	Model 1 (All)	Model 2 (Wives)	Model 3 (Husbands)
BENEFIT	-.131	-.023	-.322*
	(-.135)	(-.024)	(-.335)
EDUC	-.147	-.015	-.310*
	(-.267	(-.030)	(-.610)
MAGE	.004	.078	-.253
	(.002)	(.043)	(-.129)
SIZE	-.112	.110	-.410*
	(-.106)	(.117)	(-.353)
CLOSE	-.016	-.052	-.043
	(-.008)	(-.037)	(-.019)
R^2	.024	.012	.131

* $P < .05$.
Unstandardized estimates in parentheses.

Among the three models, Model 3 (only husband respondents) revealed substantially higher explanatory power than the other two. The five predictors explained about 13 percent of variations in fertility deviancy (R_2=.131), much more than that in the models for wives (R_2=.012) and for all respondents (R_2=.024). Stated differently, husbands' educational attainment, expectations of benefits from children, age at first marriage, family sizes of origin, and relations with their parents, all combined, can better predict deviant fertility than the same determinants for their wives.

In addition to the overall fit of the models, some interesting findings are revealed. The impact of expectations of benefits from children, which was negligible in Model 1 and 2, became significant in Model 3. The expectation factor exhibited negative effects on deviant fertility when other variables were controlled (ß=-.322). Husband respondents who had high expectations of benefits from children were less likely to involve deviant fertility than those with low expectations. This tendency was not true for the wife counterparts. In addition, a husband's educational attainment was also a significant predictor of deviant fertility (ß=-.310). Those husbands with low educational levels were more likely than those with high educational achievement to be associated with deviant fertility, controlling other related factors. Moreover, the influence of the number of siblings in a husband's family of origin on deviant fertility was also negative and significant (ß=-.410). Those husbands from small families of origin were more likely involved with deviant fertility. Consequently, in controlling other variables, family sizes of origin was the most important factor predicting deviant fertility among the husbands in the survey.

Table 5.10 presents results from the other two regression models, one with the control of previous female births and the other without. In the comparison of Model 1 and Model 2, it was found that, by including previous female births, the explanatory power in the second model increased dramatically. The impact of previous female children on deviant fertility was significantly positive (ß=.514), suggesting that respondents whose previous children were all female were likely to have deviant fertility.

Table 5.10
Logistic Regression Coefficients of Deviant Behavior by Fertility-related Variables,
Controlling Previous Female Births, OASS Data

Variables	Model 1		Model 2	
	Standardized Estimate	Parameter Estimate	Standardized Estimate	Parameter Estimate
BENEFIT	-.180	-.110	-.068	-.069
EDUC	-.190	-.202	-.109	-.203
LIVING	.005	.005	.011	.011
MAGE	.023	.012	.067	.035
SIZE	-.095	-.091	-.043	-.041
CLOSE	-.005	-.003	.065	.034
ALLGIRL			.514***	1.96***
R^2	.016		.151	

* $P < .05$;
** $P < .01$;
*** $P < .001$.

Total N = 440 individual respondents.

RESULTS OF ANALYZING IDFS DATA

Bivariate Findings

Zero-order relationships among selected variables of the IDFS data were examined by bivariate analyses. In this section, correlations between deviant fertility and all independent variables were inspected first, followed by the examination of associations among the independent variables.

Table 5.11 presents correlations between deviant fertility and socioeconomic indicators at both individual and county levels. It was evident that socioeconomic development, including both individual socioeconomic status and macro socioeconomic conditions, was significantly related to deviant fertility. Specifically, county-level productivity (r=-.187), industrialization (r=-.217), and educational levels (r=-.192) were negatively associated with deviant fertility, indicating that those respondents living in less developed areas were likely to have more children. In addition, monetary input into family planning efforts at the county-level also showed a moderate but significant relation with deviant fertility at the individual level (r=-.046). Those who lived in the area with high monetary input per person in family planning were less likely to have deviant fertility.

Similarly, individual socioeconomic status was also strongly associated with fertility deviance. As shown in the table, educational levels of both responding women and their husbands (r=-.212 and r=-.121, respectively) and occupational prestige (r=-.196 and r=-.161, respectively) were significantly correlated to deviant fertility. Moreover, family annual income was negatively associated with deviant fertility. The results suggest that married couples with high individual socioeconomic status were less likely than those with low socioeconomic status to exhibit deviant fertility.

Significant relationships were also found between deviant fertility and residence (r=.124), type of employment (r=-.214), and parents' educational levels (r=-.167). Those respondents who resided in urban regions, who worked in state-owned sectors, and whose parents had high educational levels were less likely than others to have deviant fertility.

Table 5.11

Zero-Order Correlations Between Deviant Fertility and County-Level and Individual-Level Variables on Socioeconomic Status and Family Background, IDFS Data

	Deviant Fertility
Productivity (PRODCTY)	-.187***
Industrialization (INDUSTRY)	-.217***
Educational Level (EDUCLVL)	-.192***
Monetary Input (MONEY)	-.046***
Education (EDUC)	-.212***
Husband's Education (HEDUC)	-.121***
Occupational Prestige (OCCUP)	-.196***
Husband's occupational Prestige (HOCCUP)	-.161***
Family Income (INCOME)	-.115***
Residence (RURAL)	.124***
Type of Employment (EMPLOYER)	-.214***
Parents' Education (PAMAEDUC)	-.167***

* P < .05;
** P < .01;
*** P < .001.

Correlations between deviant fertility and variables on marriage and reproductive experiences are presented in Table 5.12. As expected, early ages at first marriage were related to deviant fertility (r=-.129), and the relationship between living with parents after marriage and deviant fertility was significant (r=.112). In other words, fertility deviance was more likely to be related to those who married at an early age and those who lived with their parents after the marriage.

Table 5.12

Zero-Order Correlations Between Deviant Fertility and Variables on Marriage and Reproductive Experiences, IDFS Data

	Deviant Fertility
Age at Marriage (MAGE)	-.129***
Living with Parents (LIVEWITH)	.112***
Child Death (DEADCHD)	.024
Failed Pregnancy (FAILPREG)	.054***
Previous Female Births (ALLGIRL)	.108***

* P < .05;
** P < .01;
*** P < .001.

Table 5.12 also shows that failed pregnancy, not due to birth control purposes, was associated with deviant fertility significantly (r=.054). The relationship between child death and deviant fertility, however, was not statistically significant. A significant correlation was found between previous female births and deviant fertility (r=.108), suggesting that respondents who had all female children before the last child by the year of 1987 were likely to have deviant fertility.

As shown in Table 5.13, variables on family planning pressures and traditional influences were related to deviant fertility in the expected directions. All indicators of traditional family ideal were associated significantly with deviant fertility. The stronger the traditional family influences on an individual, the more likely the deviant fertility. More specifically, respondents who had arranged marriage by parents or others (r=.045), who shared the traditional desire of large family sizes (r=.317) and the ideal of early marriage (r=.069), and who preferred a son for the next child (r=.155), were more likely to have deviant fertility.

Table 5.13

Zero-Order Correlations Between Deviant Fertility and Variables on Family Planning Pressures and Traditional Family Influences, IDFS Data

	Deviant Fertility
Knowledge on Birth Control (KNOW)	-.129***
Abortion Because of Family Planning (ABORT)	-.114***
Discuss with Husbands (DISCUSS)	-.135***
Personal Contact by FP Personnel (CONTACT)	-.025
Arranged Marriage (ARRANGE)	.045**
Ideal of Large Family Sizes (LARGE)	.317***
Ideal of Early Marriage (EARLY)	.069***
Son Preference for Next Child (SONPREF)	.155***

* P < .05; ** P < .01; *** P < .001.

Data in Table 5.13 also reveal that the knowledge of birth control (r=-.129) and the number of abortions due to family planning (r=-.114) were correlated significantly with deviant fertility, implying that the more respondents knew about birth control measures and the more they had abortions because of family planning, the less likely they were to have deviant fertility. In addition, a significant relationship was found between fertility deviance and discussions with husbands (r=-.135). Those respondents who discussed with their husbands about the number of children they wanted were less likely to have deviant fertility than those who failed to participate in fertility discussions. Surprisingly, the relationship between personal contacts by local family planning representatives and deviant fertility was negligible.

Correlations among independent variables were further examined. Table 5.14 demonstrates significant associations between the three indicators of county-level socioeconomic developments and individual socioeconomic status (r=.380, .386, and .360 respectively) as well as between the three indicators and monetary input in family planning (r=.285, .192, and .264 respectively). The respondents living in better socioeconomic conditions were likely to enjoy higher individual socioeconomic status. Moreover, macro social and economic development was significantly related to monetary input in family planning of the areas. The higher the level of socioeconomic development, the more money allocated per person for family planning.

Table 5.14

Zero-Order Correlations Between Structural Variables on Socioeconomic Development and Individual Socioeconomic Status as well as Monetary Input in Family Planning, IDFS Data

	Socioeconomic Status (SES)	Monetary Input (MONEY)
Productivity (PRODCTY)	.380***	.285***
Industrialization (INDUSTRY)	.386***	.192***
Educational Level (EDUCLVL)	.360***	.264***

P < .05; ** P < .01; *** P < .001.

Socioeconomic development was also associated with variables on marriage and reproductive experiences, as shown in Table 5.15. Age at first marriage was significantly correlated with both individual socioeconomic status (r=.283) and macro socioeconomic conditions (r=.289). In other words, early marriage was strongly associated with lower levels of social and economic development. People with lower socioeconomic development not only married earlier, but also tended to live with their parents after the marriage. This was true for both individual status (r=-.219) and socioeconomic conditions at county-level (r=-.195).

Table 5.15

Zero-Order Correlations Between Socioeconomic Indicators and Variables in Marriage and Reproductive experiences, IDFS Data

	Individual-level	County-level
	Socioeconomic Status (SES)	Socioeconomic Condition (MACROSEC)
Age at Marriage (MAGE)	.283***	.289***
Living with Parents (LIVEWITH)	-.219***	-.195***
Child Death (DEADCHD)	-.144***	-.058***
Failed Pregnancy (FAILPREG)	.042***	.052***

* P < .05;
** P < .01;
*** P < .001.

Again in Table 5.15, indicators of unfortunate reproductive experiences were significantly correlated with socioeconomic development, but in a contradictory manner. Terminated pregnancy not due to family planning (r=.042 and .052, respectively) exhibited positive relations with socioeconomic development, while child death was negatively correlated with social and economic status (r=-.144 and -.058, respectively). These results suggest that respondents with low socioeconomic status were more likely to experience children's death and less likely to experience failed pregnancies caused by illness or other reasons than family planning.

Table 5.16 presents relationships between traditional influence indicators and related factors. There are several findings that must be noted. First, socioeconomic development variables were negatively related to traditional influences. Respondents with low socioeconomic status were likely to have arranged marriages (r=-.170), to accept the traditional ideal of large family sizes (r=-.402) and early marriage (r=-.144), and to prefer a son for the next child (r=-.249). Second, rural residents were significantly associated with arranged marriages (r=.104), the desire of large family sizes (r=.364), the ideal of early marriage (r=.156), and son preference (r=.231). The same pattern was also found for those who were employed outside the state-owned sector and those whose parents had lower levels of education attainment. Third, those respondents who married at early ages were also likely to have arranged marriages (r=-.075), the desire of large family sizes (r=-.328), son preference (r=-.113), and, of course, the ideal of early marriage (r=-.230). Similarly, living with parents after marriage was significantly related to the traditional pressures in terms of arranged marriage (r=-.032), the desire of large family sizes (r=.183), the ideal of early marriage (r=.045), and son preference (r=.141). Finally, reproductive experiences in terms of child death and failed pregnancy were positively related to arranged marriages (r=.046), the desire of large family sizes (r=.127), and the ideal of early marriage (r=.071). Failed pregnancy not due to family planning was associated with the desire of large family sizes (r=.057) as well as the ideal of early marriage (r=.039).

Based on the data presented in Table 5.16, it was evident that those respondents living in rural areas, with low socioeconomic status and less educated parents, working outside the state-owned sector, marrying at early ages, living with parents after marriage, and experiencing child death and failed pregnancy were likely to be influenced by the traditional fertility and family constraints.

Indicators of family planning pressures were further examined with relation to the same factors. As shown in Table 5.17, knowledge of

Table 5.16

Zero-Order Correlations Between Traditional Ideal Variables
and Related Factors, IDFS Data

	Arranged Marriage (ARRANGE)	Large Size Family (LARGE)	Early Marriage (EARLY)	Son Preference (SONPREF)
Socioeconomic Condition (MACROSEC)	-.117***	-.323***	-.171***	-.236***
Socioeconomic Status (SES)	-.170***	-.402***	-.144***	-.249***
Residence (RURAL)	.104***	.364***	.156***	.231***
Type of Employment (EMPLOYER)	-.081***	-.316***	-.103***	-.231***
Parents' Education (PAMAEDUC)	-.075***	-.223***	-.047***	-.150***
Age at Marriage (MAGE)	-.075***	-.328***	-.230***	-.113***
Living with Parents (LIVEWITH)	.032**	.183***	.045***	.141***
Child Death (DEADCHD)	.046***	.127***	.071***	.037
Failed Pregnancy (FAILPREG)	.003	.057***	.039***	-.025

* P < .05;
** P < .01;
*** P < .001.

contraception was positively associated with socioeconomic development at both individual (r=.516) and county-levels (r=.323). Moreover, urban residence (r=-.443) and state-owned employment (r=.406) were also strongly correlated with knowledge of birth control. Parents' educational levels were related to knowledge of birth control in a positive direction (r=.222). In addition, the respondents who married at later ages (r=.177) and did not live with parents-in-laws after marriage (r=-.212) knew more about family planning methods than their counterparts. It was also found that child death was negatively related to knowledge of family planning (r=-.060), while failed pregnancy was correlated with the knowledge positively (r=.081).

Similarly, abortion because of family planning was found to correlate with socioeconomic development at both individual and county levels (r=.212 and 203, respectively), with residence (r=-.237), with type of employment (r=.206), with parents' education (r=.094), with age at marriage (r=.177), with living with parents (r=-.128), and with failed pregnancy (r=-.039). In other words, the respondents in the survey who resided in urban regions, who had a high socioeconomic status, whose parents were more educated, who worked in the state-owned sector, who married at later ages and did not live with their parents-in-law after marriage, and who experienced terminated pregnancy not due to family planning were likely to have an abortion for birth control purposes.

Data presented in Table 5.17 further exhibited significant relationships between fertility discussions with husbands and the related variables. Socioeconomic development at both the individual level (r=.228) and the county level (r=.112) was positively associated with discussions of fertility between husbands and wives. Also, the table shows that urban residents were more likely to participate in fertility discussions within families (r=-.160) than rural ones. Also, state-owned employment (r=.169), parents' education (r=.109), and age at first marriage (r=.144) were all positively correlated with fertility discussions. Living with parents after marriage (r=-.088) and child death (r=-.091) were negatively related to fertility discussions.

Unlike other indicators in family planning, contacts by local birth control personnel were only significantly associated with individual socioeconomic

Table 5.17

Zero-Order Correlations Between Family Planning Pressure Variables
and Related Factors, IDFS Data

	Knowledge On Birth Control (KNOW)	Abortion Due to Birth Control (ABORT)	Discuss With Husbands (DISCUSS)	Contact by Birth Control Personnel (CONTACT)
Socioeconomic Condition (MACROSEC)	.323***	.203***	.112***	-.007
Socioeconomic Status (SES)	.516***	.212***	.228***	.035**
Residence (RURAL)	-.443***	-.237***	-.160***	-.007
Type of Employment (EMPLOYER)	.406***	.206***	.169***	-.024*
Parents' Education (PAMAEDUC)	.222***	.094***	.109***	-.002
Age at Marriage (MAGE)	.177***	.055***	.144***	.135***
Living with Parents (LIVEWITH)	-.212***	-.128***	-.088***	.007
Child Death (DEADCHD)	-.060***	-.011	-.091***	-.074***
Failed Pregnancy (FAILPREG)	.081***	-.039***	-.011	-.053***

* $P < .05$;
** $P < .01$;
*** $P < .001$.

status at a moderate magnitude (r=.035). The relationship between age at first marriage and the contact of family planning personnel was positive and significant (r=.135). Furthermore, unfortunate reproductive experiences in terms of child death (r=-.074) and failed pregnancy (r=-.053) were negatively related to contacts by family planning representatives, indicating that the respondents who were pursued individually by family planning agents after their marriages were less likely to have child deaths and failed pregnancies not due to birth control.

Results in Table 5.17 can be summarized as that the respondents living in urban areas, with high socioeconomic status and more educated parents, working in the state-owned sector, marrying at later ages, and not living with parents after marriage were likely to be related to the influence of family planning.

Multivariate Findings

Based on the bivariate findings, multivariate analyses were conducted. The ordinary least squares (OLS) regression technique was performed.[11] Deviant fertility was first regressed by five separate groups of variables and, then, all the variables combined. Next, models from urban and rural samples were compared. Finally, predictions for deviant fertility and the number of children were presented.

Model 1 in Table 5.18 displayed the effects of societal factors of socioeconomic conditions, monetary input in family planning, and parents' education on deviant fertility. After the other two variables were controlled, macro socioeconomic conditions had strong negative impact on deviant fertility (ß=-.201), followed by parents' educational attainment (ß=-.128). Those respondents who lived under poor socioeconomic conditions and came from families with less educated parents were likely to have deviant fertility. However, the impact of monetary input on deviant fertility, found in the bivariate analyses, became insignificant and negligible after the other two

---

[11] It is suggested by a growing body of research that results of OLS are comparable to those from logistic analysis when the range of the dependent dichotomy is between .25 and .75 and the samples are large (Knoke, 1975; Miethe, 1987).

variables were controlled. The coefficient of determinant (R^2) of .066 indicates that about 6.6 percent of the variation in deviant fertility was explained by the three predictors in the model.

Table 5.18

Standardized Regression Coefficients of Deviant Fertility
by Fertility Related Factors in Six Models, IDFS Data

	Model 1	Model 2	Model 3	Model 4	Model 5	Model 6
MACROSEC	-.201***					-.104***
MONEY	.023					.018
PAMAEDUC	-.128***					-.062***
SES		-.193***				-.091***
RURAL		-.040				-.121***
EMPLOYER		-.131***				-.091***
MAGE			-.111***			-.015
LIVEWITH			.092***			.017
DEADCHD			.014			-.008
FAILPREG			.056***			.061***
ALLGIRL			.099***			.078***
KNOW				-.091***		.043*
ABORT				-.082***		-.025
DISCUSS				-.118***		-.054***
CONTACT				.005		-.010
ARRANGE					.024	.005
LARGE					.314***	.227***
EARLY					.008	-.005
R^2	.066	.070	.039	.038	.100	.150

* P < .05;
** P < .01;
*** P < .001.

The second model demonstrated the effects of individual socioeconomic status, residence and type of employment on deviant fertility. Consistent with the results of the bivariate analyses, low socioeconomic status was significantly associated with deviant fertility (ß=-.193). Furthermore, state-owned employment had a significantly negative effect on deviant fertility (ß=-.131) after the other two variables were taken into account. Overall, these three variables explained seven percent of the variation in deviant fertility.

Indicators of marriage and reproductive experiences were included in Model 3. Age at first marriage exhibited a negative effect on deviant fertility (ß=-.111), while living with parents after marriage (ß=.092), failed pregnancy (ß=.056), and previous female births (ß=.099) had significantly positive influences. As a whole, explained variations of deviant fertility by the five predictors were slightly less than four percent.

Four variables associated with family planning pressures were introduced into Model 4. After the other factors were controlled, knowledge of contraception (ß=-.091), abortions for birth control purposes (ß=-.082), and fertility discussions (ß=-.118) revealed significant effects on deviant fertility. The findings indicated that the knowledge of contraception, abortions due to family planning, and fertility discussions between husbands and wives were negatively related to deviant fertility, even after other family planning variables were taken into account. The directions of the effects were consistent with the zero-order correlations presented earlier. Again, individual contacts by family planning personnel failed to show a statistically meaningful influence on deviant fertility. All independent variables in Model 4 could explain less than four percent of variations in deviant fertility.

Model 5 showed the effects of traditional influences on fertility deviance. Since son preference for next birth was limited only to those who wanted to have a child in the future, the variable was excluded in the multiple regression model in order to avoid a reduction in the number of cases. Among the remaining factors, the ideal of large family sizes showed a strong positive relationship with deviant fertility (ß=.314) when arranged marriage and the ideal of early marriage were held in constant. About 10 percent of variations in deviant fertility were explained by the three independent variables in the model.

Compared with the previous models, it was obvious that Model 5 had more explanatory power in predicting deviant fertility than the other models.

Model 6 in Table 5.18 included all of the variables used in Model 1 through 5. The ideal of large family sizes was the most important factor (ß=.227), followed by rural residence (ß=-.121), and county-level socioeconomic conditions (ß=-.104). It is interesting to note that rural residence, which was not statistically significant in Model 2, became the second important independent variable in Model 6. This might result from the fact that rural residence variable was significantly correlated with other independent factors such as traditional ideal of large family sizes, county-level socioeconomic conditions and fertility discussions. Additionally, individual socioeconomic status (ß=-.091), state-owned employment (ß=-.091), and parents' educational level (ß=-.062) were found to retain their significantly negative effects on deviant fertility.

The effects of age at marriage and living with parents after marriage became insignificant and negligible after the other variables were taken into account in the model. Moreover, failed pregnancy continued to show its significant impact on deviant fertility (ß=.061), and the same was true for previous female births (ß=.078). In comparison to Model 4, it was found in Model 6 that the effect of fertility discussions on deviant fertility was reduced but remained significant (ß=-.054) after other variables were controlled. However, the significant effect of abortion due to family planning found in Model 4 became trivial in Model 6 after the other factors were controlled. The overall coefficient of determination (R^2) was .150, indicating that 15 percent of variation in deviant fertility were explained by all the variables in Model 6.

Given that fertility discussions and the ideal of large family sizes were important predictors of deviant fertility when other variables were controlled, two multiple regression models were examined to assess the extent to which the related indicators affect fertility discussions and the ideal of large family sizes among Chinese women. Results are presented in Table 5.19. It was revealed that individual socioeconomic status (ß=.159) and state-owned employment (ß=.065) exhibited significantly positive effects on fertility discussions, while the influences of these two variables on the ideal of large family sizes were

negative. It is also interesting to note that the impact of contacts by family
planning personnel on fertility discussions was positive and significant
(ß=.155), suggesting that family planning pressure on individual couples may
initiate or encourage their discussions about how many children they want to
have.

Table 5.19

Standardized Regression Coefficients of Fertility Discussions and Ideal of
Large Family Sizes by Fertility Related Factors, IDFS Data

| | Dependent Variables | |
	DISCUSS	LARGE
MACROSEC	.011	-.159***
PAMAEDUC	.031	-.070
SES	.159***	-.165***
RURAL	-.019	.157***
EMPLOYER	.065***	-.086***
CONTACT	.155***	-.107***
R^2	.079	.232

* P < .05;
** P < .01;
*** P < .001.

Table 5.20 presents the results of two separate regression models in order to
predict deviant fertility by desegregating rural areas from urban areas.
Although previous studies suggested that rural and urban fertility patterns
might be different in China (Aird, 1981; Zeng and Vaupel, 1989), the same
variables were still used for both rural and urban populations in this study in

order to obtain some baseline information about the effects on deviant fertility for the two samples. Given the high correlation between the type of employment and residence, employment as an independent factor in the previous regression analyses was eliminated in the present equation. As indicated in the table, several findings are revealing. First, parents' educational levels had a significant effect on deviant fertility for the rural population (ß=-.078), but not for the urban regions (ß=.013). In other words, parents' low educational level was related to deviant fertility only in the rural areas.

Table 5.20

Standardized Regression Coefficients of Deviant Fertility by
Fertility Related Factors, Controlling Residence, IDFS Data

	Rural	Urban
MACROSEC	-.078***	-.156***
MONEY	.007	.049
PAMAEDUC	-.078***	.013
SES	-.073***	-.142***
MAGE	-.006	-.045
LIVEWITH	.022	.039
DEADCHD	.000	-.072*
FAILPREG	.050**	.067*
ALLGIRL	.046**	.245***
KNOW	.040*	.014
ABORT	-.012	-.057
DISCUSS	-.069***	-.015
CONTACT	.001	-.035
ARRANGE	-.006	.042
LARGE	.202***	.296***
EARLY	.004	-.053
R^2	.099	.361

* $P < .05$; ** $P < .01$; *** $P < .001$.

The second interesting result consisted in the differential effects of fertility discussions on deviant fertility between rural and urban couples. Discussions with husbands on the number of children had a significantly negative impact on deviant fertility in rural areas (ß=-.069). Rural respondents who participated in fertility discussions with their husbands after marriage were less likely to be identified with deviant fertility. The effect, however, became insignificant for the urban sample (ß=-.015).

The third important result involved the consistency between the rural and urban samples in terms of impact of the ideal of large family sizes, failed pregnancy, and socioeconomic development on deviant fertility. It was noted that for both rural and urban respondents the ideal of large family sizes was the most important factor predicting deviant fertility (ß=.202 and ß=.296, respectively). In addition, the significant influence of failed pregnancy on deviant fertility remained for both the rural (ß=.050) and urban samples (ß=.067). Social and economic development at county-level and individual-level exhibited significant effects on fertility for both rural and urban areas.

Finally, the coefficients of determination (R^2) of the two models displayed different explanatory powers in explaining deviant fertility. Slightly more than 36 percent of the variation in deviant fertility was explained by the 16 variables for the urban area. The explanatory strength diminished dramatically for the rural sample with the same predictors under control (R^2=.099). This result indicates that the established model for predicting deviant fertility fits better for the urban area than that for the rural one.

Table 5.21 presents the standardized regression coefficients of predicting deviant fertility and the number of children. Although deviant fertility and the number of children were highly correlated, some significant differences between the two models were uncovered when deviant fertility and the number of children were separately regressed on the same independent factors. First, consistent with the results from the OASS data analyses, age at first marriage had a significant impact on the number of children (ß=-.085), but failed to show a statistically meaningful effect on deviant fertility (ß=-.015) when the other variables were controlled. Early marriage may lead to a large number of children, but deviant fertility was unrelated to age at first marriage, statistically speaking. Second, type of employment, which had significant influences on deviant fertility (ß=-.091), did not show a statistically meaningful relation to the number of children (ß=-.036) when the other factors were controlled. Those respondents who worked in non-state-owned sectors did not have a large number of children, but were more likely to exhibit deviant fertility. Third, when the 18 variables were controlled to predict the number of children, almost 29 percent of the variation could be explained by the model. The regression equation for deviant fertility, however, only explained 15 percent of the variation. The comparison of the two models revealed that the variables were able to predict the number of children better than deviant fertility.

Table 5.21

Standardized Regression Coefficients of Deviant Fertility and Number of Children by Fertility Related Factors, IDFS Data

	Number of Children	Deviant Fertility
MACROSEC	-.045*	-.104***
MONEY	.011	.018
PAMAEDUC	-.057***	-.062***
SES	-.136***	-.091***
RURAL	.051**	-.121***
EMPLOYER	-.036	-.091***
MAGE	-.085***	-.015
LIVEWITH	.010	.017
DEADCHD	.012	-.008
FAILPREG	.076***	.061***
ALLGIRL	.127***	.078***
KNOW	.097***	.043*
ABORT	.064***	-.025
DISCUSS	-.070***	-.054***
CONTACT	-.003	-.010
ARRANGE	.010	.005
LARGE	.322***	.227***
EARLY	.000	-.005
R^2	.289	.150

• $P < .05$; ** $P < .01$; *** $P < .001$.

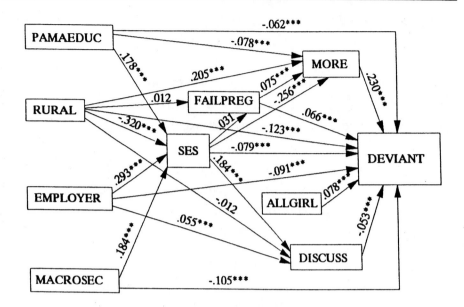

Figure 5.6　Path Model of Fertility-Related Factors on Deviant Fertility, IDFS Data

Path Analysis

Following the bivariate and multivariate analyses, a path analysis was performed. The major advantages of path analysis consist in setting up a causal framework and allowing the disaggregation of associations into components as direct, indirect, or spurious effects (Wolfle, 1980; 1989). Accordingly, a path model was established and illustrated in Figure 5.6. All the variables which were statistically significant at .001 level in the previous multiple regressions were included in the path model. Specifically, parents' education (PAMAEDUC), rural residence (RURAL), state-own employment (EMPLOYER), county-level socioeconomic condition (MACROSEC), and previous female births (ALLGIRL) were exogenous variables, while the endogenous variables of individual socioeconomic status (SES), failed pregnancy (FAILPREG), the ideal of large family sizes (LARGE), and discussions with husbands (DISCUSS) and deviant fertility (DEVIANT) were included in the model. Path coefficients were estimated and presented in Figure 5.6.

As shown in the figure, when the ideal of large family sizes was presented, parents' educational levels (ß=-.078), rural residence (ß=.205), failed pregnancy (.075), and socioeconomic status (ß=-.256) demonstrated significant influences. Both socioeconomic status (ß=.184) and state-owned employment (ß=.055) were significantly related to fertility discussions with husbands. The impact of rural residence, however, was not statistically significant (ß=-.012) when the other two factors were under control.

As deviant fertility is the major endogenous variable, the direct and indirect effects of the selected factors on deviant fertility are decomposed and exhibited in Table 5.22. The composition of the effects on deviant fertility extends the knowledge obtained from the previous multiple regression analyses.

Table 5.22

The Total, Direct, and Indirect Effects of Fertility-related Variables
on Deviant Fertility, IDFS Data

Variables	Total Effect	Direct Effect	Indirect Effect	Correlation
PAMAEDUC	-.106	-.062	-.044	-.167
RURAL	-.028	-.123	.095	.124
EMPLOYER	-.136	-.091	-.045	-.214
MACROSEC	-.118	-.105	-.013	-.226
SES	-.139	-.079	-.060	-.244
FAILPREG	.083	.066	.017	.054
ALLGIRL	.078	.078	na	.108
DISCUSS	-.053	-.053	na	-.135
LARGE	.230	.230	na	.317

na = not applicable

First, the direct effect of rural residence on deviant fertility was negative, but its indirect effects on deviant fertility were positive (.095). As shown in the model, rural residence had positive indirect influences on deviant fertility through socioeconomic status (.025), failed pregnancy (.001), the ideal of large family sizes (.047), and discussions with husbands (.001). Among them, the indirect paths through socioeconomic status and the ideal of large family sizes contributed substantially to deviant fertility. The results indicated that rural residents were more likely to hold the traditional ideal of large family sizes (ß=.205), which, in turn, affected deviant fertility positively (ß=.230). Moreover, rural residents were more likely to have lower socioeconomic status (ß=-.320), and low socioeconomic status was related to deviant fertility (ß=-.079). Because the insignificant effects of rural residence on failed pregnancy, the impact of rural residence on deviant fertility through failed pregnancy was very weak.

Second, the total effect including both the direct (-.062) and indirect ones (-.044) was able to account for the majority of the correlation (r=-.167) between parents' education and deviant fertility. The negative influence of parents' education on deviant fertility came from the paths that pass through individual socioeconomic status and the ideal of large family sizes. These findings indicated that the negative impact of parents' education was partially caused by the connections between parents' education and their socioeconomic status, which in turn resulted in the ideal of large family sizes and deviant fertility.

Third, individual socioeconomic status affected deviant fertility both directly (-.079) and indirectly (-.060). Nevertheless, it is interesting to note that socioeconomic status affected deviant fertility positively through failed pregnancy, but negatively through the ideal of large family sizes and fertility discussions with husbands. The strongest indirect impact came through the path from socioeconomic status to the ideal of large family sizes to deviant fertility.

In short, the decomposition of effects in the path model provided an alternative for further exploring the relationships previously discovered. Also the path analysis explored the relationships in a causal order and specified the effects of independent variables by different paths.

CHAPTER VI

SUMMARY AND DISCUSSION

SUMMARY

Findings from Descriptive Analyses

The Records of County Family Planning Commission (RCFPC) provided the official version of birth counts and incidences of deviant fertility in the area. The three-year records illustrated several facets related to the main focus of this study.

First, deviant fertility is officially defined as those "out-of-plan" second-order births and births in third or higher order. According to the data, approximately 45 percent of the total births from 1988 to 1990 were second or higher order births. Among the second order births, which comprised 32 percent of the total births, about 72 percent were approved by the government while 28 percent were deviant fertilities. The data also showed that the components of "out-of-plan" births were largely dependent on family planning policies. After the policy allowed some couples to have their second children, many couples did so with or without permission. It is plausible that many second-order births had been justified as "planned" while they were actually not. Often, people used bribes and faked certificates to change a second-order birth from "out-of-plan" to "planned" (World Journal, 1992).

The second finding consisted in a great increase in third or higher order births from 1988 to 1989. The majority of deviant fertility in 1989 came from the third or higher order births. This phenomenon occurred primarily due to the policy adjustments in 1988. Although the new policy, which allowed rural daughter-only-households to have a second birth, was introduced earlier in Guangdong, it was not until 1988 then the policy officially included all rural areas of the country. Since early 1989 a universal "two-children-with-spacing" policy has been practiced in the rural areas of Guangdong (Zeng, 1989). Despite the fact that the third or higher order births were prohibited even under the new policy, the overall relaxed regulation might encourage some couples to go one step further and to have more than two children.

Finally, the distribution of pregnancies and outcomes revealed that only a small number of "out-of-plan" pregnancies result in "out-of-plan" births. This appeared attributable to family planning policies that required women with "out-of-plan" pregnancies to undergo abortions (Aird, 1986; Kaufman et al., 1989). Under the influence of family planning propaganda and regulations, couples with "out-of-plan" pregnancy might either have an abortion voluntarily or be forced to do so. In addition, the availability and accessibility of abortion facilities in China might also contribute to the results.

Descriptive analyses of both the IDFS and the OASS data also portrayed some important tendencies in deviant fertility. Although findings from the IDFS and the OASS data are not identical in some aspects, some general patterns and trends are revealing. First, the majority of fertility deviants married during the 1970s when the "Later-Longer-Fewer" family planning regulations were in effect; they might not violate the family planning rules of the 1970s but might do so in the 1980s. The longer the time after the marriage, the more likely that the deviant tendency resulted in fertility. On the other hand, it might be speculated that some of those who married in the 1980s, especially after the mid 1980s, had not conflicted with the family planning regulations only because of the matter of time.

The final notable finding in the descriptive analysis concerned the relationship between deviant fertility and social and economic conditions. At least in the IDFS data, fertility deviants were likely to be those who lived in rural areas, had low educational attainment, and had low family incomes. Although it was true that "wealthy" families could pay "penalties" for their deviant births, fertility deviants, as a group, were likely to have low socioeconomic status.

Findings from OASS Data

The Old-Age Security Survey (OASS) data were analyzed by using both bivariate and multivariate statistical techniques. The independent variables included expectations of benefits from children, living standards, family sizes of origin, relations with parents, previous female births, and educational attainment.

The analyses uncovered a number of fascinating results with relation to deviant fertility in China. Perhaps the most important finding is the strong relationship found between deviant fertility and the gender of previous children. Data showed that deviant fertility was significantly related to the number of daughters but not to the number of sons. Also, multiple regression analyses demonstrated that the respondents with all female children were more likely to have a deviant birth. The factor of previous female births was the most important predictor affecting deviant fertility when the other variables were controlled. These results may reflect the fact that Chinese couples violate the family planning regulations simply because they want to have a son. After they have a son, they are inclined to limit their fertility. If they have only female children, however, many couples tend to violate the family planning policies no matter how many children they have already had.

Second, it is also interesting to note that some variables associated with the number of children may not be necessarily related to deviant fertility. For example, consistent with the previous literature, age at first marriage was significantly correlated with the total number of living children, but was not significantly related to deviant fertility. This result may provide evidence for the claim that studying deviant fertility in China is unique and should not be equated with general fertility studies in which the number of children has been emphasized.

The third important finding in this section involved the differences between husbands and wives in the sample with respect to the predictive patterns for deviant fertility. Although wives demonstrated higher expectations of benefits from children than their husband counterparts, the expectation was not a significant predictor of deviant fertility among wives. Furthermore, the results of logistic regressions for husbands revealed that the effect of educational attainment on deviant fertility was negative and significant. It was also found that husbands' family sizes of origin exhibited a significant impact on deviant fertility. A similar pattern did not appear for wives, which suggests a possible gender difference in the issue of deviant fertility in China.

Finally, the analyses of the OASS data also revealed that parents' expectations of benefits from children varied with their educational attainment and family sizes of origin. High expectations of benefits from children were significantly associated with those parents with low educational levels and those originally from large families. Moreover, it was interesting to note that expectations of benefits from children were a function of the gender of children rather than the number of children. With the increase of the number of sons, expectations of benefits from children went up. The expectation declined while the number of female children increased. These findings provide additional evidence of strong preference for sons to daughters, which is associated with deviant fertility in China.

Findings from IDFS Data

The In-Depth Fertility Survey (IDFS) provides an important data source for this study, due not only to its sufficient sample size but also to a variety of variables relevant to the topic. The analysis of data used 28 variables and utilized such statistical techniques as Pearson's correlation, multiple regression, and path analysis.

The initial findings consisted in significant zero-order relationships found in bivariate analyses. It became evident that deviant fertility was significantly related to socioeconomic characteristics, at both the individual and county levels. Educational attainment of parents was also negatively associated with deviant fertility. In addition, those respondents who resided in rural areas and did not work in the state-owned sector were more likely than others to be identified with fertility deviance.

The relationships between deviant fertility and indicators of marriage and reproductive experiences were also significant. Specifically, deviant fertility was negatively related to age at marriage, and positively correlated with living with parents after marriage, failed pregnancy, and previous female births. Furthermore, age at marriage was positively related to socioeconomic characteristics, and the relationship between socioeconomic development and living with parents after marriage was negative and statistically significant.

The second set of findings involved selected indicators of constraints from traditional and current fertility norms. It was found that, in general, indicators of current family planning pressures were negatively associated with deviant fertility, while significantly positive associations were found between fertility deviance and traditional family norm constraints. It was also interesting to discover that these traditional pressure indicators were significantly related to low socioeconomic status, rural residence, non-state-owned employment, low educational attainment of parents, and living with parents after marriage. On the other hand, indicators of family planning constraints, such as knowledge of birth control, abortions due to family planning, and participation in fertility discussions with husbands, were significantly associated with higher socioeconomic status, higher educational attainment of parents, urban residence, state-owned employment, and not living with parents after marriage.

The third collection of findings resulted from the multivariate analyses of the IDFS data. After all the relevant variables were controlled in the multiple regression model, the remaining meaningful factors were county-level socioeconomic conditions, education of parents, individual socioeconomic status, area of residence, type of employment, failed pregnancy, previous female births, fertility discussions with husbands, and the ideal of large family sizes. These factors have significant effects on deviant fertility at the .001 level, even after other variables were taken into account.

The fourth notable result from the IDFS data was the differences between the rural and urban samples in terms of the effects of individual variables on deviant fertility and different explanatory powers of the models. The established regression model for predicting deviant fertility appeared more suitable for the urban sample than the rural one. In addition, educational attainment of parents, which exhibited a significant impact on deviant fertility in the rural model, failed to demonstrate its meaningful effect in the urban sample. Fertility discussions with husbands significantly affected deviant fertility for rural residents, but did not produce a significant influence for urban ones. These results provide evidence that the area of residence not only strongly affects the dependent variable, but also manifests interactive effects on other variables that in turn influences deviant fertility.

The fifth major finding of the IDFS data consisted in the comparison of predicting the number of children and deviant fertility. The finding is somewhat consistent with that from the OASS data. Although there exists a great deal of similarity between predicting the two dependent variables, the difference appears more striking. When the same factors were under control, non-state-owned employment was significantly related to deviant fertility, but did not lead to a large number of children. Age at first marriage had a significant impact on the number of children, but its effect on deviant fertility was negligible. The comparison further supports the postulation that there may be discrepancies in predicting deviant fertility and number of children.

Finally, the path analysis uncovered a number of particular paths through which deviant fertility is affected. Among them, the indirect effects of residence on deviant fertility are worth mentioning. Rural residence demonstrated relatively strong influences on deviant fertility through socioeconomic status and the ideal of large family sizes. And much of the negative impact of parents' education on deviant fertility was also obtained by the paths through socioeconomic status and the ideal of large family sizes. Thus, it can be concluded that individual socioeconomic status and traditional desires for more children served as crucial factors in transmitting the indirect effects of residence and parents' education to deviant fertility.

Summary of Hypothesis Tests

The nine hypotheses formulated earlier were tested in the data analyses. The results of the tests were summarized and listed as follows.

	Hypothesis	Test Results
Hypothesis 1:	Chinese couples who have strong traditional norm constraints of fertility are more likely to have deviant fertility than those couples who do not have strong traditional pressures.	Supported by the IDFS data
Hypothesis 2:	Chinese couples who are strongly constrained by new family planning norms are less likely to have deviant fertility than those couples who are not significantly limited by the new fertility norms.	Partially supported by the IDFS data
Hypothesis 3:	Chinese couples who have unfortunate reproductive experiences are more likely to be involved with deviant fertility than those who don't have the experiences.	Supported by the IDFS data
Hypothesis 4:	Chinese couples who have only female children are more likely than those who had previous male offspring to commit fertility deviance.	Strongly supported by both the IDFS and OASS data
Hypothesis 5:	Chinese couples who live with their parents, especially parents on the husband's side, are more likely to have deviant fertility than other couples.	Not supported by the OASS data, partially supported by the IDFS data
Hypothesis 6:	Chinese couples who enjoy high socioeconomic status are more likely to be constrained by current family planning norms than those couples with low socioeconomic status.	Strongly supported by the IDFS data
Hypothesis 7:	Chinese couples who reside in rural areas are more likely than those living in cities to accept traditional fertility ideals and have deviant fertility.	Strongly supported by the IDFS data

	Hypothesis (Cont'd)	Test Results (Cont'd)
Hypothesis 8:	Chinese couples who grew up in families with low socioeconomic status are more likely to be influenced by traditional family ideals than those who came from better-off families.	Partially supported by the IDFS data
Hypothesis 9:	Chinese couples who are personally contacted by family planning personnel are more likely to follow the new reproductive regulations than those couples who are not strongly approached by family planning programs.	Not supported by the IDFS data

INTERPRETATION AND DISCUSSION

Given the richness of the results in this study, it is difficult to address all the findings. This section, however, will cover a number of major results of the study and discuss them in terms of the relationships between deviant fertility and rural-urban differences, son preference, women's status, and fertility norm conflicts in China.

Rural-Urban Differences and Deviant Fertility

One of the main findings consists in the discrepancies between rural and urban areas in relation to the traditional ideal of large family sizes and, in turn, to deviant fertility. The results parallel the fact that urban and rural fertility patterns and levels are different in China (Aird, 1981; Yi and Vaupel, 1989). A knowledge of social and structural distinctions between rural and urban regions appears necessary to understand this issue.

China is an agricultural nation and three out of every four Chinese are rural residents (The State Statistical Bureau, 1990). For years, however, the Chinese government has implemented many social and economic policies that give the urban sector additional privilege. In China, as in many other developing countries, the wide gap in income and opportunities between farmers and urban residents constitutes the great inequality between rural and urban population. In relation to the economic disadvantages, rural areas also suffer from the lack of welfare systems supported by the state.

Unlike their urban counterparts who can receive pensions after retirements, rural residents in China depend mainly upon supports of their children when they grow old. The agricultural collective's guarantees of food, shelter, clothing, medical care and burial, so called "five guarantees," provide only minimal aids for the elderly, and by no means can substitute the economic and emotional supports provided by one's own children (Chen and Kols, 1982; Davin, 1985; Davis-Friedmann, 1985). For rural peasants, having enough surviving children is extremely important, not only for maintaining their family lines, but also for their old-age security. Thus, rural families have a greater demand for surviving children than their urban counterparts. It is expected that the strong demand for enough children for old-age supports will not diminish until adequate old-age security systems are developed in rural China. Consequently, the phenomenon of deviant fertility is likely to continue.

The desire for more children by rural families is also the result of rational calculations in terms of economic advantage. A family is the main productive unit in rural China, which has been enhanced since the rural reform in 1979. Under the new "family responsibility system," land previously owned by communes is divided and contracted to individual families. Households want to expand their labor force in order to increase the yield from their lands. The normal way for a family to enlarge their labor force, however, is to increase the number of family members. Therefore, the dependency period for Chinese children in rural villages is brief; children usually engage in such economic activities as feeding livestock, caring for their younger siblings and helping in the fields at an early age. Parents' benefits from the additional work force and the advantages of a large family seem apparent.

As in other nations, Chinese urban areas are characterized by such factors as high population density, high industrialization, and high costs of living. These characteristics of urban life imply higher social and economic costs associated with childbearing and childrearing. It is estimated that the cost of raising a child in large cities of China is more than four times the cost in rural villages. For urban young couples living on low wages, having children is bound to have a negative effect on their standard of living. In addition, for many years housing in cities was allocated according to social status and types of employment rather than to actual needs. Having more children creates housing problems for young couples with low socioeconomic status. Given the pressure of urban life, urban residents may be more easily convinced about the negative effects of a large family and population growth than their rural counterparts. As a result, urban couples in China are more likely than rural ones to accept the family planning regulations and to distance themselves from fertility deviance.

In addition to the structural factors mentioned earlier, educational attainment appears relevant to rural-urban differences in deviant fertility. It is often the case in China that urban residents are more likely to have higher educational levels than rural villagers. Caldwell regards education as an institutional factor influencing fertility behavior by changing the direction of wealth flow between generations (Caldwell, 1982; Cutright, 1983). On the one hand, the improvement in education of both parents and children increases the costs of childbearing and childrearing. On the other hand, educated parents are more likely than uneducated ones to accept the fact that education reduces their children's availability to work. But how does the education of a couple's parents make a difference in their fertility behavior? Based on the results of this study, two connections may be considered. First, parents' education levels are closely related to the couples' socioeconomic status, which is negatively associated with deviant fertility. Second, parents' education may affect the couples' traditional fertility ideals and attitudes and thereafter fertility deviance. Education, not only of a married couple and their children but also of their parents, is an important factor influencing the couple's fertility behavior.

One related finding in this study is that educational attainment by parents is more likely to influence deviant fertility among rural couples, while the impact of urban parents' education seems negligible. Two possible interpretations appear appropriate. First, the influences of the old generations over the young are more evident in rural areas than in cities. It is perhaps due to the fact that modern nuclear families are more prevalent in cities than in rural villages (Tien and Lee, 1988; Zeng, 1986). The lack of co-residences reduces the interactions between generations. As a result, the impact of traditional ideals held by the older generation to the young is likely to be diminished. Another possible explanation consists in the fact that urban youth are more likely to be exposed to modern lifestyles than the rural youth, regardless of family formats. The growing availability of modern means of career advancement, communication, and entertainment allows the young generation to adopt a modern lifestyle rapidly and spontaneously. Consequently, the gap between the young generation and the old widens. The influence of parents' preferences concerning family sizes and fertility seems less likely to pass to the young couples despite the fact that they may live in the same household.

Furthermore, rural-urban differences in deviant fertility may also stem from the distinct social control applied to cities and villages. Social control in China has relied heavily upon the authority of social resources. Urban employees, especially those who work in the state-owned sector, enjoy high privilege at the cost of strict control by the Chinese government. The power over housing allocation, job promotions, career mobility and even family matters makes the urban residents more susceptible to state policies and regulations. For them the punishments for violating family planning rules are much more severe and effective. Compared to that of their urban counterparts, the life of rural villagers looks more autonomous. In spite of the tight ideological dominion, rural peasants are somewhat free from certain sanctions. In the case of family planning programs, rural couples who have "out-of-plan" children may be subject to fines, but their behavior may not influence their career moves and living conditions. As some peasants became "rich" since the rural reform in 1979, it is often the case that those rich peasants are more than happy to "buy" their extra children. Thus it is easier for rural couples than urban ones to manifest their traditional large family desires in their fertility behavior.

The Chinese government implements more moderate birth control measures in rural areas than in cities. But these moderate policies cannot lessen the strong traditional fertility norms that are prevalent among rural villagers. Indeed, disparity in socioeconomic developments of rural and urban regions is the most important factor contributing to the rural-urban differences in deviant fertility.

The relationship between socioeconomic development and fertility has been a classic topic among social demographers since the inception of the demographic transition theory. Although China has been used as an example to illustrate the difficulty of applying the transition theory to a developing and agricultural nation where a dramatic fertility decline occurs (Kaufman, 1983; Aird, 1981; Mauldin, 1982), a growing body of studies suggests that China follows the general pattern described by the transition hypothesis (Birdsall and Jamison, 1983; Li and Ballweg, 1992; Platte, 1984; Poston and Gu, 1987; Tien, 1984). However, it should be admitted that the demographic transition theory does not provide an answer to the question of how socioeconomic situations influence individual fertility behavior. For years many scholars have tried to offer a solution by identifying some intermediate links connecting fertility and socioeconomic factors. Freedman (1979) suggests that social and economic factors first change the norms of people and thereafter the norms affect a series of intermediate variables that can have impacts on fertility behavior. This explanation can shed light on the understanding of the relationships between socioeconomic conditions and deviant fertility. The present study further provides evidence that socioeconomic status does influence fertility behavior through reproductive norms and desires.

Son Preference and Deviant Fertility

One major finding of this study is that those couples who have only female children are more likely to engage in deviant fertility than those who already have a son. This reflects the fact that Chinese couples violate the family planning regulations simply because they want to have a son. In other words, son preference is a very important determinant of deviant fertility in China.

The traditional Chinese family was patriarchal, patrilineal, and patrilocal. Only sons were permanent members of their parents' family. The family line passed through sons, and male offspring were symbolically important for the family and kinship. The patriarchal family structure and the resulting strong son preference became an institutionalized value. According to the tradition, a man's duties to his ancestors include having a son and therefore guaranteeing that the family name would survive. Thus, to have at least one son and preferably many sons was regarded as necessary for a family.

Today, in spite of the official condemnation, the tradition that sons fulfill symbolic function is still evident in most parts of China and particularly in rural areas and among couples of low socioeconomic status (Arnold and Liu, 1986). In many rural areas, the patrilocal system perseveres and patriarchal beliefs are still pervasive. Almost immutably daughters still move to their husband's villages and responsibility for caring for parents continues to rest primarily on male children and their wives. Therefore, in addition to the son preference tradition, having sons proves more advantageous than having daughters in rural China. For instance, a greater economic return may be expected by parents from sons than from daughters, simply because sons tend to remain at home longer than daughters. Given the society with gender differentiation in work, sons are often considered by their parents as more productive than daughters. Moreover, in the absence of a proper social welfare system in rural China, the only way that rural peasants feel secure about their old age is to have at least one son to take care of them later on. Although those urban residents who work in the state-owned sector can enjoy an old-age pension system, these people only comprise about 10 percent of the total population. For most Chinese, especially those rural Chinese, old-age security is a family obligation. Thus, until an old-age security system is universally provided, rural parents will remain dependent on their children in the future. For some of them, the new official family planning norms may simply be unacceptable.

As stated earlier, both the continuing influence of the traditional ideals and the lack of a developed welfare program in rural areas contribute to the continuance of son preference in China. Actually, the phenomenon of son preference has not attracted much attention for a long time until it became a major source of resistance to the current family planning policy. The strict family planning regulations in China would result in many couples having no sons. Given the symbolic and practical importance of having a son for rural families, average peasant couples may not be ready to limit their fertility if their previous children are female. Under such circumstances, the desire for a son may become even stronger because of the limited number of births imposed by the family planning regulations. With the powerful preference of sons, it is likely that many rural couples will want to keep having children until they have a son.

In additional to deviant fertility, son preference is also related to other deviant behavior such as female infanticide, abandonment of female children, and abuse of women who give birth to daughters, just to name a few. The skewed sex ratios at birth in 1980s supported the previous suspicions on the occurrence of female infanticide and abandonment in China (Hull, 1990; Johansson and Nygren, 1991; Kristof, 1991). With the limitation of having one or two children, some couples are reluctant to "waste" their quota on daughters. Therefore, many baby girls become "unwanted," and even abandoned or killed. Furthermore, son preference may also result in the reality that girls receive less care and attention than boys in many Chinese families, which reduces the chance of survival of baby girls.

The preference for sons to daughters is widespread and persistent in China. Although the examination of the traditional ideals, the current social system, and the responses to family planning policies shed light on the issue, a full understanding of this phenomenon and its relations to deviant fertility should go beyond these aspects. After all, the persistence of son preference in China reflects the inferior status of Chinese women.

Chinese Women's Status and Deviant Fertility

Although many Chinese women prefer to have a son rather than a daughter, they are also victims of the son preference. In China women are often mistreated because they give birth to a girl. One letter written by fifteen women who had given births to daughters read:

Whatever it takes, even at the cost of our lives, we women still want to have sons . . . Why would we risk our lives to do this bitter thing which endangers the nation and us? Because in our village, if a woman does not have a son, she suffers from discrimination and mistreatment which are even greater in its bitterness than this risking our lives (People's Daily, 1983).

Women in feudalist China had probably the most brutal oppression in the human history. Foot-binding, child bride, concubinage, and girl infanticide were only parts of the miserable lives of Chinese women. Under the Confucian ideology, a set of codes of ethics regulated women's conducts. For instance, the "three obedience" defined the subordination of women to men. A woman should be obedient to her father and brothers when young, obedient to her husband when married, and obedient to her sons when widowed (Andors, 1983). Indeed, the Confucian customs constituted the foundation of male supremacy in China.

There is no doubt that the lack of women's rights and progress leads to the point that women themselves are likely to have a strong motivation for giving births to sons. Women not only need sons to contribute security in old age, but more importantly they need sons to gain status in their families and communities (Johnson, 1983). It is customary in rural China that only those women who have at least one son are considered as "complete" and those who do not have a son are often prejudged and discriminated against by the whole community. Therefore, as long as the traditional marriage patterns and structures continue viewing women as outsiders in their husbands' families and communities, women will continue to rely on their male children as a primary source of membership, influence, and status in the family and community.

Since 1949, substantial efforts have been made by the government to improve the status of Chinese women. Women are referred as "half the sky" and supposed to be equal to men in terms of equal opportunity for education, labor force participation, and pay. Nevertheless, gender equality is by no means a reality in today's China. Differences have been found in leadership position, education, and employment (Arnold and Liu, 1986; Croll, 1983; Dalsimer and Nisonoff, 1987; Hemmel and Sindbjerg, 1984; Hong, 1987). In spite of more and more women becoming economically self-supporting, most leadership positions are held by men. Recent statistical data reveal that about 93 percent of leaders at the provincial level and 94 percent at the county level, are males (World Journal, 1991). In terms of education, women make up 70 percent of the illiterates in China, and approximately 80 percent of children who do not attend primary schools are girls. Lower educational attainment further prevents women from working in many relatively desirable jobs. In fact, women tend to concentrate in low prestige occupations such as service, commerce, and agriculture, and are under represented in governmental and professional occupations (Li, 1989).

Since female offspring have much less potential than male counterparts to benefit the family both economically and symbolically, it is not surprising that the tradition of son preference powerfully persists and that deviant fertility is prevalent in China. It is a woman who gives birth to a child. Her reproductive behavior may be blamed for not having a son in a family and be punished for violating current family planning regulations by the government. Women are indeed the victims. In the long run, deviant fertility further hinders the improvement of women's status. While those baby boys who are considered as "out-of-plan" by the government policy are likely to bring joy to the families, the "out-of-plan" girls may not be welcome by both the government and the parents. Those girls are often kept in hiding, given up for adoptions, or simply abandoned. It is estimated that a significant number of female births may never be reported to the authorities (Tien, 1992). Consequently, these girls will be further denied appropriate medical and health care as well as education and employment opportunities in the future. More importantly, their miserable experiences may turn into a strong son preference by those women, because they will desperately need sons to improve their status. This unfortunate circle implies that, as long as women are still in the inferior position, the son preference becomes inevitable and, in turn, deviant fertility is likely to occur in China.

What can be done? The findings of this study provide some insights on this issue. It is found that those women who participated in fertility discussions with their husbands on how many children they want are less likely to have deviant fertility than those women who fail to engage in fertility discussions with their husbands. Actually, fertility discussions between a wife and a husband can be considered as the process of decision-making, which is closely related to the power structure within the family. It is generally assumed that, since women sacrifice more than men during childbearing and childrearing, the more a wife involves herself in the decision-making of fertility, the more likely she will end up with a small number of children. Some evidence suggests that Chinese women desire fewer children than their husbands and in-laws (Johnson, 1983;

Parish and Whyte, 1978). Yet the impact of their desires on actual fertility is quite limited. Fact is that a Chinese woman, especially from a rural area, lacks power in decision-making on the matters of family and clan because she is only a marginal member. A husband may consult with his parents about how many children he should have rather than discuss the matter with his wife. It is suggested that increased gender equality in families, which would increase women's participation in fertility discussions, might lead Chinese couples to limit their family sizes in China.

It is supported in this study and a related research that women's socioeconomic development helps to participate in fertility discussions in the family (Li, 1993). Improvement in women's socioeconomic status, especially educational attainment, influences women's desire for children and their traditional mother roles. However, these attitude changes may not manifest themselves in fertility behavior unless women are able to participate actively in fertility decision-making within the family. One policy strategy suggested by this study is to encourage women to become active in fertility discussions. In doing so, women's support groups may be practical in the short term, and improvement in women's educational attainment and other opportunities will be effective in the long run.

Fertility Norm Conflicts and Deviant Fertility

The major focus of this study is to use a fertility norm conflict approach to understand deviant fertility in China. This approach proves beneficial in terms of examining the large-scale societal picture rather than accusing individuals. Reproductive behavior of an individual is quite personal and private in its natural form. Nevertheless, like other types of human behavior, fertility behavior does not occur in a vacuum but in a social context. The fundamental norms that guide the behavior and the social meanings attached to the behavior constitute the social significance in the issue of deviant fertility.

It is generally agreed that the success of the Chinese family planning programs largely depends on the effort to persuade those of childbearing age to accept family planning measures and establish new family planning norms. However, it is unrealistic to expect newly established fertility norms to suddenly replace the traditional norms concerning family sizes. In fact, the new reproductive norms exist side by side with the traditional fertility ideals. The conflict between the two is rather intense in China.

The large family ideal has been a characteristic of Chinese culture for several thousand years. The traditional thoughts such as "the more children, the more happiness," "no descendants means no filial piety," and "bringing up the children today in order to have someone to rely on in old age" are deeply rooted in Chinese culture and lifestyles (Beijing Review, 1982; Sun and Wei, 1987). Traditionally, the ideal of a large family with many children, especially sons, is a fundamental norm directing people's fertility behavior.

Traditional Chinese fertility norms of a large family and son preference directly conflict with the new official reproductive norms imposed by the family planning programs. Chinese family planning programs have relied heavily upon ideological efforts. During the family planning campaigns, the propaganda machines in China are at full operations. Individual families and couples are required to sacrifice their own interests for social obligations and the collective benefits for the country. There is no doubt that the ideological propaganda does introduce and reinforce the new family planning norms to individuals. Nevertheless, norm changes in a society are rather gradual and do not parallel ideological reformations. Especially in the situation where collective pursuits somewhat conflict with the interests of individual couples such as old-age security, the new official norm of small family sizes may not be internalized to guide people's fertility behavior, but rather become a coercive measure. On the other hand, traditional fertility norms are likely to remain effective through social interaction within intimate groups and communities, which appear to shape individual perceptions and behavior more persistently than some compulsory means.

Furthermore, changes of fertility norms require corresponding structural transformations. In fact, the fertility patterns in China have been susceptible to its social and institutional changes. For instance, the conflicts between family planning norms and traditional fertility ideals become more intense after the rural economic reforms known as the "production responsibility system" began in the early 1980's. The reform shifts the unit of management and accounting from production teams to peasant families. Under the new system, households are responsible for economic production and the private wealth of families. While agricultural production rapidly increases, so too does the economic value of children. Rural families choose to bear more children and pay the economic penalties, calculating that the benefit of more children outweighs the costs (Banister, 1984; Croll, 1983). Moreover, as indicated earlier, the traditional ideals of large family sizes and son preference are facilitated within current social institutions and structures in China. Although these conventional ideals threaten the goals of family planning programs, they are likely to continue unless institutional changes occur. The structural changes suggested in this study include socioeconomic development, the establishment of appropriate old-age security systems in rural areas, and the improvement of women's status in general and women's power within families and communities in particular.

The conflict between the traditional fertility ideals and the new reproductive norms imposed by the government family planning programs can also be understood in terms of relativity of norm conformity. In complex societies, normative agreement seems very problematic because of the diversity of competing values. The differences of fertility norm definitions in China exist not only between individual and collective interests, but also among people with various family backgrounds, socioeconomic status, and their early reproductive experiences.

Another implication of this study is related to the influences of Chinese family planning programs on deviant fertility. This study does not provide evidence of how family planning efforts, either monetary input on family planning or contacts by family planning personnel, have reduced deviant fertility in China. Nevertheless, it is suggested in this study that family planning pressures imposed upon individual couples may affect their fertility discussions. The contacts by family planning personnel may encourage a husband and a wife to confront and discuss the issue of family sizes and planning. Also, it is noted that contacts by family planning personnel may reduce the traditional ideal of large family sizes. In this way, people's fertility is likely to be planned.

In conclusion, deviant fertility is indeed a complex social phenomenon. The coexistence and conflict between the traditional fertility ideals and the new family planning norms often put individual couples into a difficult situation of decision making. The normative conflict on fertility and family sizes is the key to understanding deviant fertility in China. This study, as a primary effort, demonstrates the uniqueness of analyzing deviant fertility from a sociological perspective, which cannot be replaced by general fertility research with the focus on the number of children. Previous fertility studies had usually treated fertility as a whole, revealing fertility determinants that are supposed to suit everyone in a population. However, the demands or the reasons for having children caused by a variety of fertility determinants may be sufficient to explain normal, but not deviant, fertility. There are substantial differences between normal fertility and deviant fertility in the sense that normal fertility behaves within socially approved ranges while deviant fertility is in opposition to socially valued expectations. The fertility norm conflict approach presented in this study is helpful because it examines a large-scale societal picture rather than focusing on individuals.

Limitations and Recommendations

A major limitation of this study comes from the secondary data analysis. The In-Depth Fertility Survey was designed primarily to examine the general patterns and trends of fertility in China. Only limited attention was paid to fertility desires, let alone the motivation of violating the current fertility regulations. Similarly, the Old-Age Security Survey was also restricted by its original blueprint with limited questions related to fertility desires and behavior.

Given that the empirical examinations of this study are patterned by what is already available in the data sets, some concepts developed earlier cannot be measured and tested in a satisfactory fashion. For instance, the pressure of traditional fertility norms was only measured by separate items in the survey. The ideals of large family sizes, arranged marriage, son preference, and early marriage were used to measure various dimensions of the traditional influences. Because of the differences in responding categories of the survey questions, these aspects could not be combined into a single factor. In a similar manner, family planning pressure was also measured by individual items and the operational definition may be limited to the problem of measurement error.

Deviant fertility is a new concept. The measurement of the concept is complicated, taking into account the indicators of the number of living children, family planning regulations, rural-urban variations, time and types of marriage, and majority-minority differences. However, the measurement can be improved by considering the physical and mental conditions of previous children. According to the family planning policy, a couple is allowed to have another child if their previous child is disabled and has serious defects. Without the relevant questions available in the survey, this study could not identify this situation.

The integration of individual and county-level variables may result in some questionable outcomes. Given the limited variations at the county-level, the aggregated individual-level variables were also restricted. Relatively speaking, relations between indicators with more variation are more likely to be statistically significant than between those with less variation. This may be the reason for the weak relationship between the county-level monetary input on family planning and deviant fertility.

Another question consideration goes to the analysis of the Old-Age Security Survey data. The survey questioned husbands and wives separately. Thus, it is legitimate to consider them as individual respondents. However, the results should be interpreted with caution. Interdependence between husbands and wives may exist in such variables as perceived living conditions, age at first marriage, and educational attainment. It is possible that the interdependent situation may lead to distorted results.

Additionally, the causal ordering of variables in the path analysis may also be questioned. For instance, it is assumed that individual socioeconomic status influences deviant fertility. It is also possible to argue that fertility deviance may result in the low status. It perhaps makes sense to say that failed pregnancy appears related to ideal of large family sizes and thereafter deviant fertility. It is also possible to assume that the experience of having more children may lead to more failed pregnancies. The debatable linkage order in the path analysis does not mean that the analyses are spurious, but that the interpretation requires more evidence in the future research, especially through longitudinal studies on this issue.

Based on the multiple regression analysis, the relevant control variables can explain about 15 percent of the variation in deviant fertility for the whole sample. The majority of the variation remains unexplained. It is expected that some important factors are still excluded in the study. Future studies may solve the problem by conducting surveys focusing on deviant fertility and establishing more comprehensive models for predicting deviant fertility.

The final recommendation consists in the theoretical framework of deviant fertility. The results of the study suggest the benefits of conceptualizing deviant fertility in a norm conflict approach. It looks also promising, however, if the issue is explored by using other theoretical perspectives. For example, social labeling theory may help to examine the stigma attached to those Chinese couples who violate the family planning regulations. Also, the phenomenon of deviant fertility may be explained by the means-end perspective of deviance, which regards having enough children or sons as a means for realizing the end of old-age security. Deviant fertility is a complex social reality and its causes are multiple. Clearly, a better understanding of this topic requires more comprehensive theoretical perspectives and research in the future.

BIBLIOGRAPHY

Adnan, Shapan. 1982. "Conceptualizing Fertility Trends in Peripheral Formations." Pp.203-224 in *Determinants of Fertility Trends: Theory Re-Examined,* edited by Charlette Hohn and Rainer Mackensen. Belgium: IUSSP.

Adler, Nancy E. 1979. "Decision Models in Population Research." *Journal of Population* 2(3): 187-202.

Aird, John. 1981. "Fertility Decline in China." Pp. 119-227 in *Fertility Decline in the Less Developed Countries.* New York, NY: Praeger Publishers.

Aird, John. 1986. "Coercion in Family Planning: Causes, Methods, and Consequences." pp. 184-221 in *China's Economy Looks Towards the Year 2000: The Four Modernizations,* edited by US Joint Economic Committee. Washington, D.C.: US Government Printing Office.

Andors, Phyllis. 1983. *The Unfinished Liberation of Chinese Women, 1949-1980.* Bloomington: Indiana University Press.

Arnold, Fred and Zhaoxiang Liu. 1986. "Sex Preference, fertility, and Family Planning in China." *Population and Development* Review 12(2): 221-246.

Banister, Judith. 1984. "Population Policy and Trends in China, 1978-1983." *China Quarterly* 100: 717-741.

Banister, Judith. 1987. *China's Changing Population.* Stanford, CA: Stanford University Press.

Beach, Lee R., Brenda D. Townes, Frederick L. Campbell, and Gordon W. Keating. 1976. "Developing and Testing a Decision Aid for Birth Planning Decisions." *Organizational Behavior and Human Performance* 15: 99-116.

Becker, Gary S. 1960. "An Economic Analysis of Fertility." Pp. 209-240 in *Demographic and Economic Change in Developed Countries*, edited by University-National Bureau Committee for Economic Research. Princeton: Princeton University Press.

Becker, Gary S. 1965. "A Theory of the Allocation of Time." *The Economic Journal* 75: 493-517.

Becker, Gary S. 1988. "Family Economics and Macro Behavior." *The American Economic Review* 78(1): 1-13.

Beijing Review. 1982. "Rural Population." Pp. 181-183 in "On Population and Population Policy in China." *Population and Development Review* 9(1): 181- 184.

Birdsall, Nancy and Dean T. Jamison. 1983. "Income and Other Factors Influencing Fertility in China." *Population and Development Review* 9(4): 651-675.

Bongaarts, John. 1978. "A Framework for Analyzing the Proximate Determinants of Fertility." *Population and Development Review* 4: 105- 132.

Bongaarts, John. 1985. "An Alternative to the One-Child Policy in China." *Population and Development Review* 11(4): 585-617.

Bryant, Clifton D. 1990. *Deviant Behavior: Readings in the Sociology of Norm Violation*. New York: Hemisphere Publishing Corporation.

Bulatao, Rodolfo A. 1982. "Value of Children." Pp. 665-671 in *International Encyclopedia of Population* Vol.2, edited by J. A. Boss. New York: The Free Press.

Bulatao, Rodolfo A. and Fred Arnold, 1977. "Relationships Between the Value and Cost of Children and Fertility: Cross-Cultural Evidence." Pp. 141-156 in *Proceeding of the International Population Conference, Mexico City*. Liege, Belgium: IUSSP.

Bulatao, Rodolfo A. and Ronald D. Lee. 1983. "An Overview of Fertility Determinants in Developing Countries." Pp. 757-786 in *Determinants of*

Fertility in Developing Countries Vol.2, edited by Rodolfo A. Bulatao and Ronald D. Lee. New York: Academic Press.

Buripakdi, C. 1977. *The Values of Children: A Cross-National Study, Thailand*, Vol. 4. Honolulu, East-West Population Institute.

Burch, Thomas K. 1980. "Decision-making Theories in Demography: An Introduction." Pp. 1-22 in *Demographic Behavior: Interdisciplinary Perspectives on Decision-Making*, edited by Thomas K. Burch. Boulder, Co: Westview Press.

Caldwell, John C. 1982a. *Theory of Fertility Decline*. London: Academic Press.

Caldwell, John C. 1982b. "The Wealth Flows Theory of Fertility Decline." Pp. 169- 188 in *Determinants of Fertility Trends: Theory Re-Examined,* edited by Charlette Hohn and Rainer Mackensen. Belgium: IUSSP.

Caldwell, John C. 1987. "Toward a Restatement of Demographic Transition Theory." Pp. 42-69 in *Perspectives on Population: An Introduction to Concepts and Issues*, edited by Scott W. Menard and Elizabeth W. Moen. New York: Oxford University Press.

Cancian, Francesca M. 1975. *What Are Norms? A Study of Beliefs and Action in A Maya Community*. London: Cambridge University Press.

Chan, Kam Wing and Xueqiang Xu. 1985. "Urban Population Growth and Urbanization in China Since 1949: Reconstructing a Baseline." *China Quarterly* 104: 583-613.

Chen, Muhua. 1980. "Speak at Family Planning Meeting." *People's Daily*, February 14, 1980.

Chen, Muhua. 1981. "Birth Planning in China." Pp. 71-78 in *Research on the Population of China: Proceedings of a Workshop*, edited by Robert J. Lapham and Rodolfo A. Bulatao. Washington, D.C.: National Academy Press.

Chen, Pichao and Adrienne Kols. 1982. "Population and Birth Planning in the People's Republic of China." *Population Reports* 25: 577-618.

China's State Statistical Bureau. 1987. *China's In-Depth Fertility Survey Program*. Beijing: Department of Population Statistics at State Statistical Bureau.

Clay, Daniel C. and James J. Zuiches. 1980. "Reference Groups and Family Size Norms." *Population and Environment* 3: 262-279.

Coale, Ansley J. 1973. "The Demographic Transition." Pp. 53-72 in *International Population* Conference, Vol. 1. Liege, Belgium: UISSP.

Coale, Ansley J. 1984. "The Demographic transition." *The Pakistan Development Review* 23(4): 531-552.

Congress of the United States. 1982. "Evolution of China's Birth Planning Policy." Pp. 205-219 in *World Population and Fertility Planning Technology: The Next 20 Years.* Washington, D.C.: U.S. Government Printing Office.

Croll, Elisabeth. 1983. *Chinese Women Since Mao.* New York: M.E. Sharpe.

Croll, Elisabeth. 1983. "Production Versus Reproduction: A Threat to China's Development Strategy." *World Development* 11(6): 467-481.

Croll, Elisabeth. 1985. "Introduction: Fertility Norms and Family Size in China." Pp. 1-36 in *China's One-Child Family Policy*, edited by Elisabeth Croll, Delia Davin and Penny Kane. New York: St. Martin's Press.

Croll, Elisabeth, Delia Davin and Penny Kane. 1985. *China's One-Child Family Policy.* New York: St. Martin's Press.

Cutright, Phillips. 1983. "The Ingredients of Recent Fertility Decline in Developing Countries." *International Family Planning Perspectives* 9(4): 101-109.

Dalsimer, Marlyn and Laurie Nisonoff. 1987. "The Implications of the New Agricultural and One-Child Family Policies for Rural Chinese Women." *Feminist Studies* 13(3): 583-607.

David, Henry P. 1982. "Incentives, Reproductive Behavior, and Integrated Community Development in Asia." *Studies in Family Planning* 13(5): 159-173.

Davin, Delia. 1985. "The Single-child Family Policy in the Countryside." Pp. 37-82 in *China's One-Child Family Policy*, edited by Elisabeth Croll, Delia Davin and Penny Kane. New York: St. Martin's Press.

Davis, Kingsley, 1959. "The Sociology of Demographic Behavior." Pp. 309-333 in *Sociology Today: Problems and Prospects*, edited by Robert K. Merton. New York: Basic Book.

Davis, Kingsley. 1963. "The Theory of Change and Response in Modern Demographic History." *Population Index* 29(4): 345-352.

Davis, Kingsley. 1984. "Wives and Work: The Sex Role Revolution and Its Consequences." *Population and Development Review* 10(3): 397-417.

Davis, Kingsley and Judith Blake. 1956. "Social Structure and Fertility: Analytical Framework.*" Economic Development and Cultural Change* 4: 211-233.

Davis, Kingsley and Pietronella van den Oever. 1986. "Demographic Foundations of New Sex Roles." Pp. 13-29 in *Fertility and Mortality: Theory, Methodology and Empirical Issues*, edited by K. Mahadevan. Beverly Hills: Sage Publications.

Davis-Friedmann, Deborah, 1985. "Old Age Security and the One-child Campaign." Pp. 149-161 in *China's One-Child Family Policy*, edited by Elisabeth Croll, Delia Davin and Penny Kane. New York: St. Martin's Press.

Department of Social Problem, 1988. "Old Security Survey of Banyu, Guangdong." Pp. 28-48 in *Research in Social Work*, edited by Luming Wang. Beijing: XueYue Publication.

Duncan, O. Dudley. 1966. "Path Analysis: Sociological Examples.*" American Journal of Sociology* 72: 1-22.

Easterlin, Richard A. 1975. "An Economic Framework for Fertility Analysis." *Studies in Family Planning* 6: 54-63.

Easterlin, Richard A. 1978. "The Economics and Sociology of Fertility." Pp. 57-134 in *Historical Studies of Changing Fertility*, edited by Charles Tilly. Princeton: Princeton University Press.

Fawcett, James T. 1970. *Psychology and Population: Behavioral Research Issues in Fertility and Family Planning*. New York: The Population Council.

Feng, Junjun. 1989. "We Don't Have Choice." *People's Daily* (Overseas Edition) April 14, 1989. p. 4.

Findlay, Allan and Anne Findlay. 1987. *Population and Development in the Third World*. New York: Methuen.

Fishbein, Martin. 1967. "Attitude and the Prediction of Behavior." Pp. 477-492 in *Readings in Attitude Theory and Measurement*, edited by Martin Fishbein. New York: John Wiley & Sons.

Fishbein, Martin. 1972. "Toward an Understanding of Family Planning Behaviors." *Journal of Applied Social Psychology* 2(3): 214-227.

Fishbein, Martin and James J. Jaccard. 1973. "Theoretical and Methodological Considerations in the Prediction of Family Planning Intention and Behavior." *Representative Research in Social Psychology* 4: 37-51.

Freedman, Ronald. 1963. "Norms for Family Size in Underdeveloped Areas." *Proceedings of the Royal Society*, Vol. 159, Series B. London: The Royal Society Burlington House.

Freedman, Ronald. 1975. *The Sociology of Human Fertility: An Annotated Bibliography*. New York: John Wiley & Sons.

Freedman, Ronald. 1979. "Theory of Fertility Decline: A Reappraisal." *Social Forces* 58(1): 1-17.

Freedman, Ronald. 1986. "Theories of Fertility Decline." Pp. 30-36 in *Fertility and Mortality: Theory, Methodology and Empirical Issues*, edited by K. Mahadvan. Beverly Hill: Sage Publications.

Fried, Ellen S. and J. Richard Udry. 1980. "Normative Pressures on Fertility Planning." *Population and Environment* 3(3,4): 199-209.

Gibbs, Jack P. 1965. "Norms: The Problems of Definition and Classification." *American Journal of Sociology* 70: 586-594.

Gibney, Frank. 1992. "China's Renegade Province: Guangdong Does Fine without Either Marx or Mao." *Newsweek,* February 17, 1992.

Greenhalgh, Susan. 1986. "Shifts in China's Population Policy, 1984-86: Views from the Central, Provincial, and Local Levels." *Population and Development Review* 12(3): 491-515.

Greenhalgh, Susan. 1989. *Fertility Trends in China: Approaching the 1990s*. Working Papers, No. 8. New York, NY: Research Division, The Population Council.

Guangdong Statistical Bureau. 1990. "Information on 1990 Census Data." *Yangcheng Evening News*, November, 9, 1990.

Guo, Shenyang. 1990. *Shanghai: Pioneer of Fertility Decline in People's Republic of China - Trends and Determinants of Fertility Transition.* Unpublished dissertation, The University of Michigan.

Gustavus, Susan O. 1973. "The Family Size Preferences of Young People: A Replication and Longitudinal Follow-up Studies." *Studies in Family Planning* 4(1-2): 335-342.

Gustavus, Susan O. and Charles B. Nam. 1970. "The Formation and Stability of Ideal Family Size Among Young People." *Demography* 7(1): 43-51.

Handwerker, W. P. 1986. "Culture and Reproduction: Exploring Micro/Macro Linkages." Pp. 1-28 in *Culture and Reproduction: An Anthropological Critique of Demographic Transition Theory,* edited by W. Penn Handwerker. Boulder, Co: Westview Press.

Hawthorn, Geoffrey. 1970. *The Sociology of Fertility.* London: The Macmillan Company.

He, Sonyan, Zhenqiu Kuang, and Bingqiang Lu. 1987. *Procedure of Sampling.* Unpublished Notes.

Hemmel, Vibeke and Pia Sindbjerg. 1984. *Women in Rural China.* London: Curzon Press.

Hendershot, Gerry E. 1969. "Familial Satisfaction, Birth Order, and Fertility Values." *Journal of Marriage and the Family* 31(1): 27-33.

Hess, Peter N. 1988. *Population Growth and Socioeconomic Progress in Less Developed Countries: Determinants of Fertility Transition.* New York: Praeger.

Hoffman, Lois W. and Martin L. Hoffman, 1973. "The Value of Children to Parents." Pp. 19-76 in *Psychological Perspectives on Population,* edited by James T. Fawcett. New York: Basic Book Publishers.

Hoffman, Lois W. and Manis, J. D. 1979. " The Value of Children in the United States: A New Approach to the Study of Fertility." *Journal of Marriage and the Family* 41: 583-596.

Hong, Lawrence K. 1987. "Potential Effects of the One-Child Policy on Gender Equality in the People's Republic of China." *Gender & Society* 1(3): 317-326.

Hull, Terence H. 1990. "Recent Trends in Sex Ratios at Birth in China."
   Population and Development Review 16(1): 63-83.
Iritani, Toshio. 1979. *The Value of Children: A Cross-National Study, Japan.*
   Vol. 6. Honolulu, East-West Population Center.
Jaccard, James J. and Andrew R. Davidson. 1972. "Toward and Understanding
   of Family Planning Behaviors: An initial investigation." *Journal of Applied
   Social Psychology* 2(3): 228-235.
Johansson, Sten and Ola Nygren. 1991. "The Missing Girls of China: A New
   Demographic Account." *Population and Development Review* 17(1): 35-51.
Johnson, Kay A. 1983. *Women, the Family and Peasant Revolution in China.*
   Chicago: The University of Chicago Press.
Jones, Gavin W. 1982. "Fertility Determinants: Sociological and Economic
   Theories." Pp. 279-285 in *International Encyclopedia of Population,*
   Vol.1, edited by J. A. Boss. New York: The Free Press.
Kane, Penny. 1985. "The Single-child Family Policy in the Cities." Pp. 83-113
   in *China's One-Child Family Policy*, edited by Croll, Elisabeth, Delia
   Davin and Penny Kane. New York: St. Martin's Press.
Kane, Penny. 1987. *The Second Billion: Population and Family Planning in
   China.* New York: Penguin Books.
Kaufman, Joan. 1983. *A Billion and Counting: Family Planning Campaigns
   and Policies in the People's Republic of China.* San Francisco, CA: San
   Francisco Press.
Kaufman, Joan, Zhang Zhirong, Qiao Xinjian, and Zhang Yang. 1989. "Family
   Planning Policy and Practice in China: A Study of Four Rural Counties."
   Population and Development Review 15(4): 707-729.
Knodel, John and Etienne van de Walle. 1979. "Lessons from the Past: Policy
   Implications of Historical Fertility Studies." *Population and Development
   Review* 5: 217-345.
Knoke, David. 1975. "A Comparison of Log-Linear and Regression Models for
   Systems of Dichotomous Variables." *Sociological Methods & Research*
   3(4): 416-433.
Kristof, Nicholas D. 1991. "Where Had All the Girls Gone?" *New York Times*
   June 30, 1991.

Lavely, William. 1986. "Age Pattern of Chinese Marital Fertility, 1950-1981." *Demography* 23(3): 419-434.

Lee, Sung Jin and Jung-oh Kim. 1977. *The Value of Children: A Cross-National Study, Korea.* Vol. 7. East-West Population Center.

Leibenstein, Harvey. 1957. *Economic Backwardness and Economic Growth.* New York: Wiley.

Leibenstein, Harvey. 1974. "An Interpretation of the Economic Theory of Fertility: Promising Path or Blind Alley?" *Journal of Economic Literature* 12(2): 457- 479.

Leibenstein, Harvey. 1975. "The Economic Theory of Fertility Decline." *Quarterly Journal of Economics* 89(1): 1-31.

Leibenstein, Harvey. 1980. "Relaxing the Maximization Assumption in the Economic Theory of Fertility." Pp. 35-48 in *Determinants of Fertility Trends: Theories Re-Examined*, edited by Charlotte Hohn and Rainer Mackensen. Belgium: IUSSP.

Li, Jiang Hong. 1989. "How Well Do Women Fare in Education and Occupation in Modern China." Paper presented at the annual meeting of the Mid-South Sociological Association, Louisiana, 1989.

Li, Li. 1993. "Chinese Women's Participation in Fertility Discussions." *International Journal of Sociology of the Family* 23(1): 33-43.

Li, Li and John A. Ballweg. 1992. "Development, Urbanization and Fertility in China." *Sociology and Social Research* 76(3): 111-117.

Liang, Jimin. 1989. "China's Family Planing Program Is Advancing." Pp. 31-41 in *International Population Conference*,Vol. 1. Belgium: IUSSP.

Lin, Nan and Wen Xie. 1988. "Occupational Prestige in Urban China." *American Journal of Sociology* 93(4): 793-832.

Ma, En. 1989. "One Child, One Family." *Journal of the American Medical Association* 261(12): 1735-1736.

Mason, Karen O. 1983. "Norms Relating to the Desire for Children." Pp. 388-428 in *Determinants of Fertility in Developing Countries*, Vol. 1, edited by Rodolfo A. Bulatao and Ronald D. Lee. New York: Academic Press.

Mauldin, Parker W. 1982. "The Determinants of Fertility Decline in Developing Countries: An Overview of the Available Empirical Evidence." *International Family Planning Perspectives* 9: 116-121.

McCaghy, Charles H. 1985. *Deviant Behavior: Crime, Conflict, and Interesting Groups*. New York: Macmillan Publishing Company.

McGregor, James. 1991. "China's Entrepreneurs Are Thriving in Spite Of Political Crackdown." *The Wall Street Journal* June 4, 1991.

McNicoll, Geoffrey. 1982. "Institutional Determinants of Fertility Change." Pp. 147-167 in *Determinants of Fertility Trends: Theory Re-Examined*, edited by Charlotte Hohn and Rainer Mackensen. Belgium: IUSSP.

Miethe, Terance D. 1987. "Stereotypical Conceptions and Criminal Processing: The Case of the Victim-Offender Relationship." *Justice Quarterly* 4(4): 301-324.

Mo, Liren. 1990. "The Difficulty of Mainland China's Population Census." *China Time Weekly* May 5-11, 1990.

Nam, Charles B. and Mary G. Powers. 1983. *The Socioeconomic Approach To Status Measurement*. Houston: Cap and Gown Press.

Namboodiri, N. Krishnan. 1986. "Social Development and Population Change - A Reappraisal of Selected Theories." Pp. 37-54 in *Fertility and Mortality: Theory, Methodology and Empirical Issues*, edited by K. Mahadevan. Beverly Hills: Sage Publications. 37-54.

Notestein, Frank W. 1945. "Population - The Long View." Pp. 36-57 in *Food For The World*, edited by Theodore W. Schultz. Chicago: University of Chicago Press.

Ory, Marcia G. 1978. "The Decision to Parent or Not: Normative and Structural Components." *Journal of Marriage and the Family* 40: 531-539

Pagel, Mark D. and Andrew R. Davidson. 1984. "A Comparison of Three Social-Psychological Models of Attitude and Behavioral Plan: Prediction of Contraceptive behavior." *Journal of Personality and Social Psychology* 47: 517- 533.

Parish, W. L. and M. K. Whyte. 1978. *Village and Family in Contemporary China*. Chicago: The University of Chicago Press.

Park, Chai Bin and Jing Qing Han. 1990. "A Minority Group and China's One-Child Policy: The Case of the Koreans." *Studies in Family Planning* 21(3): 161- 170.

Parsons, Talcott. 1951. *The Social System*. Glencoe, IL: Free Press.

People's Daily, February 23, 1983.

People's Daily, Overseas Edition, December 15, 1989.

People's Daily, Overseas Edition, September 13, 1990.

People's Daily, Overseas Edition, February 5, 1991.

People's Daily, Overseas Edition, May 21, 1991.

Platte, Erika. 1984. "China's Fertility Transition: The One-Child Campaign." *Pacific Affairs* 57: 646-671.

Population Census Office. 1991. *10 Percent Sample Tabulation on the 1990 Population Census of China*. Beijing: The State Council Department of Population Statistics of the State Statistical Bureau.

Population Census Office. 1987. *The Population Atlas of China*. Oxford: Oxford University Press.

Poston, Dudley L. Jr. and Boochang Gu. 1987. "Socioeconomic Development, Family Planning, and Fertility in China." *Demography* 24(4): 531-551.

Poston, Dudley L. Jr. and Jing Shu. 1987. "The Demographic and Socioeconomic Composition of China's Ethnic Minority." *Population and Development* 13(4): 703-722.

Potter, Joseph E. 1983. "Effects of Societal and Community Institutions on Fertility." Pp. 627-665 in *Determinants of Fertility in Developing Countries,* Volume 2, edited by Rodolfo A. Bulatao and Ronald D. Lee. New York: Academic Press.

Raina, B. L. 1969. "Family Size Norms." *Family Planning News* 10: 22-28.

Rosenstiel, Lutz von, Gunther Oppitz, and Matin Stengel. 1980. "Motivation of Reproductive Behavior: A Theoretical Concept and Its Application." Pp. 79-93 in *Determinants of Fertility Trends: Theories Re-Examined*, edited by Charlotte Hohn and Rainer Macknsen. Belgium: IUSSP.

Ryder, Norman B. 1980. "Where Do Babies Come From?" Pp. 189-202 in *Sociological Theory and Research: A Critical Appraisal*, edited by Hubert M. Blalock, Jr. New York: Free Press.

Sanderson, Warren C. 1976. "On Two Schools of the Economics of Fertility." *Population andDevelopment Review* 2(3): 469-478.

Schultz, Theodore, W. 1974. *Economics of the Family: Marriage, Children, and Human Capital*. Chicago: The University of Chicago Press.

Sellin, Thorsten. 1938. *Cultural Conflict and Crime*, Bulletin 41. Social Science Research Council.

Sun, Yingzhau and Yilei Gao. 1990. "Rural and Urban Industrialization in the People's Republic of China." *The Rural Sociologist* 10(4): 14-16.

Sun, Yuesheng and Zhangling Wei. 1987. "The One-Child Policy in China Today." *Journal of Comparative Family Studies* 18(2): 309-325.

Teitelbaum, Michael S. 1975. "Relevance of Demographic Transition for Developing Countries." *Science* 188: 420-425.

The State Statistical Bureau. 1989. "1988 Regional Population Reports." *People Daily* April 15, 1989.

The State Statistical Bureau. 1990. "On 1990 Population Census Data." *People Daily* October 31, 1990.

Thompson, Warren. 1929. "Population." *American Journal of Sociology* 34(6): 959-975.

Thomson, Elizabeth. 1984. "Subjective Utility and Plans for Childbearing and Employment." *Population and Environment* 7(3): 198-208.

Tien, H. Yuan. 1980. "Wan, Xi, Shao: How China Meets Its Population Problem." *International Family Planning Perspectives* 6(2): 65-73.

Tien, H. Yuan. 1983. *China: Demographic Billionaire*, Population Bulletin, Vol.38, No. 2. Washington, D.C.: Population Reference Bureau, Inc.

Tien, H. Yuan. 1984. "Induced Fertility Transition: Impact of Population Planning and Socio-economic Changes in the People's Republic of China." *Population Studies* 38: 385-400.

Tien, H. Yuan. 1992. "China's Demographic Dilemmas." *Population Bulletin* 47(1).

Tien, H. Yuan and Che-fu Lee. 1988. "New Demographics and Old Designs: The Chinese Family Amid Induced Population Transition." *Social Science Quarterly* 69(3): 605-628.

Tien, H. Yunan, Zhang Tianlu, Ping Yu, Li Jingneng, and Liang Zhongtang. 1982. "China's Demographic Dilemmas." *Population Bulletin* 47(1): whole issue.

Townes, Brenda D., Lee R. Beach, Frederick L. Campbell and Donald C. Martin. 1977. "Birth Planning Values and Decisions: The Prediction of Fertility." *Journal of Applied Social Psychology* 7(1): 73-88.

Townes, Brenda D., Lee R. Beach, Frederick L. Campbell, and Roberta L. Wood. 1980. "Family Building: A Social Psychological Study of Fertility Decisions." *Population and Environment* 3: 210-220.

Treiman, Donald J. 1977. *Occupational Prestige in Comparative Perspective.* New York: Academic Press.

Turchi, Boone A. 1975. "Microeconomic Theories of Fertility: A Critique." *Social Forces* 54(1): 107-125.

Udry, J. Richard. 1982. "The Effect of Normative Pressures on Fertility." *Population and Environment* 5(2): 109-122.

van de Walle, Etienn and John Knodel. 1980. "Europe's Fertility Transition: New Evidence and Lessons for Today's Developing World." *Population Bulletin* 34(6), whole issue.

Vinokur-Kaplan, Diane. 1978. "To Have-or Not to Have-Another Child: Family Planning Attitudes, Intentions, and Behavior." *Journal of Applied Social Psychology* 8(1): 29-46.

Vogel, Ezra F. 1989. *One Step Ahead in China.* Cambridge, Massachusetts: Harvard University Press.

Wang, Feng. 1987. *China's Reproductive Revolution: Individual and Community Determinants of Fertility Variation in Hebei, China.* Unpublished dissertation, The University of Michigan.

Wang, Feng. 1988. "The Role of Individuals' Socioeconomic Characteristics and the Government Family Planning Program in China's Fertility Decline." *Population Research and Policy Review* 7: 255-276.

Wang, Jichuan. 1990. *Family Planning and Fertility Transition in Shifang County, Sichuan, People's Republic of China.* Unpublished dissertation, Cornell University.

Wasserstrom, Jeffrey. 1987. "Resistance to the One-Child Family." Pp. 269-276 in *Perspectives on Population: An Introduction to Concepts and Issues*, edited by Menard, Scott W. and Elizabeth W. Moen. New York: Oxford University Press.

Weeks, John R. 1989. *Population: An Introduction to Concepts and Issues*, Fourth Edition. Belmont, CA: Wadsworth Publishing Company.

Werner, Paul D., Susan E. Middlestadt-Carter, and Thomas J. Crawford. 1975. "Having A Third Child: Predicting Behavioral Intentions." *Journal of Marriage and the Family* 37: 348-358.

Westoff, Charles F. and Raymond H. Potvin. 1966. "Higher Education, Religion and Women's Family-Size Orientation." *American Sociological Review* 31(4): 489-496.

Willis, Robert J. 1974. "Economic Theory of Fertility Behavior." Pp. 25-75 in *Economics of the Family: Marriage, Children, and Human Capital*, edited by Theodore W. Schultz. Chicago: The University of Chicago Press.

Wilson, Richard W. 1981. "Moral Behavior in Chinese Society: A Theoretical Perspective." Pp. 1-20 in *Moral Behavior in Chinese Society*, edited by Richard W. Wilson, Sidney L. Greenblatt, and Amy A. Wilson. New York: Praeger Publishers.

Wolfle, Lee M. 1980. "Strategies of Path Analysis." *American Educational Research Journal* 17(2): 183-209.

Wolfle, Lee M. 1989. "Path Analysis." Class handout for *Advanced Statistics for Education*.

World Journal, April 3, 1991a.

World Journal, May 21, 1991.

World Journal, January 19, 1992.

World Journal, March 11, 1992.

Wu, Tsong-Shien. 1977. *The Value of Children: A Cross-National Study, Taiwan*. Vol. 5. Honolulu, East-West Population Center.

Ye, Wenzhen. 1991. *The Determinants of Demand for Children, Evidence from Rural Hebei, China*, Unpublished dissertation, University of Utah.

Yu, Y.C. 1979. "The Population Policy in China." *Population Studies* 33(1): 125-142.

Zeng, Yi. 1986. "Changes in Family Structure in China: A Simulation Study." *Population and Development Review* 12(4): 675-703.

Zeng, Yi. 1989. "Is the Chinese Family Planning Program `Tightening Up'?" *Populationand Development Review* 15(2): 333-337.

Zeng, Yi and James W. Vaupel. 1989. "The Impact of Urbanization and Delayed Childbearing on Population Growth and Aging in China." *Population and Development Review* 15(3): 425-445.

Zhang, Xing Quan. 1991. "Urbanization in China." *Urban Studies* 28(1): 41-51.

Zhu, Yuncheng. 1986. *Chinese Population: Guangdong Province*. Beijing: Chinese Financial and Economic Publication.

INDEX